Praise for *WITHOUT A DOUBT*

"Surbhi Sarna is a success story, but this is no victory lap. In *Without a Doubt*, she shares the challenges faced by underrated entrepreneurs, but more importantly, she gives a plan to overcome them—and thrive."

—Arianna Huffington, founder & CEO, Thrive Global

"When it comes to doling out wisdom for entrepreneurs, *Without a Doubt* delivers."

—Andy Fang, founder of DoorDash

"*Without a Doubt* is an object lesson in resilience. Surbhi Sarna shows us how outsiders can win, if they're sufficiently resourceful and determined."

—Jessica Livingston, founder of Y Combinator and author of *Founders at Work*

"Entrepreneurs can change the world. Surbhi Sarna has done just that and in this authentic telling of her story, she shows how you can too. The book is inspiring."

—Tim Draper, venture capitalist and founder of Draper Associates

"*Without a Doubt* is a story about a girl who judo flips on her devastation and heartbreak. It is a fresh perspective and guide on company building and activism that will inspire others to help make a better world."

—Tracy Young, cofounder of Plangrid and CEO of TigerEye

"Whether people or overvaluing or undervaluing you, it doesn't matter. Surbhi Sarna shows you how to go long on yourself and get things done."

—Michael Seibel, partner at Y Combinator

"Surbhi Sarna's drive to innovate and her reluctance to quit even in the toughest of circumstances will inspire readers to chase solutions that will improve the health of the world."

—Michael Mahoney, CEO of Boston Scientific

"[An] inspiring debut . . . Budding entrepreneurs will find this a motivating, accessible entry."

—*PUBLISHERS WEEKLY*

"Perhaps as a result of the ways in which she was underestimated, Sarna's approach to entrepreneurship, which she articulates through warm and humorous advice embedded in her life story, is profoundly empathetic, both for her coworkers and community and for herself. *Without a Doubt is* a wise, practical, and compassionate guide to startup success from a determined woman."

—*KIRKUS REVIEWS* (starred review)

How to Go from Underrated to Unbeatable

WITHOUT A DOUBT

SURBHI SARNA

SIMON & SCHUSTER PAPERBACKS

New York   London   Toronto   Sydney   New Delhi

An Imprint of Simon & Schuster, LLC
1230 Avenue of the Americas
New York, NY 10020

First Simon & Schuster trade paperback edition March 2024

SIMON & SCHUSTER PAPERBACKS and colophon are registered
trademarks of Simon & Schuster, LLC

Simon & Schuster: Celebrating 100 Years of Publishing in 2024

For information about special discounts for bulk purchases,
please contact Simon & Schuster Special Sales at
1-866-506-1949 or business@simonandschuster.com.

The Simon & Schuster Speakers Bureau can bring authors to
your live event. For more information or to book an event, contact
the Simon & Schuster Speakers Bureau at 1-866-248-3049
or visit our website at www.simonspeakers.com.

Interior design by Lewelin Polanco

Manufactured in the United States of America

1   3   5   7   9   10   8   6   4   2

Library of Congress Cataloging-in-Publication Data has been applied for.

ISBN 978-1-9821-4790-7
ISBN 978-1-9821-4791-4 (pbk)
ISBN 978-1-9821-4792-1 (ebook)

For my mom and
everyone else who believed in me

For everyone who did not

Contents

Note to Readers

This book contains autobiographic details and is the product of my work and experiences. Certain names and identifying details have been changed. Certain quotes have been reconstructed from memory, to the best of my ability.

WITHOUT A DOUBT

Introduction

Being so surprised you fall out of your chair isn't just an expression. Because there I found myself, sprawled on my bedroom floor, my cheek pressed uncomfortably against the rug. Just a moment earlier, I had been sitting on the edge of my bed when I heard the chime of a new email from my laptop. Attached was a document I'd been waiting for.

It was from my investment banker, Rakesh. I held my breath and clicked on it. I had spent the last seven years working day and night to build a company called nVision Medical, creating a device that I hoped would one day catch ovarian cancer in its early stages. We were a small startup in what many would consider a niche market, developing a microcatheter that contained a delicate, cell-collecting balloon that was as thin as a spaghetti noodle. In a landscape crowded with unicorn tech companies, my startup had been frequently overlooked by venture capitalists and others. As a thirty-two-year-old female CEO, I had been dismissed as neither having the experience nor education to lead a sophisticated company in a highly regulated health care industry. I'd stumbled again and again, sometimes barely making it back onto my feet. And yet our scrappy team had persisted and eventually managed to raise enough money to complete three clinical trials, garner two FDA clearances, and obtain several patents that protected our device.

Though the product hadn't yet made a dollar, we were making progress using the venture capital we raised. We still had a lot of work to do: uncertainties to navigate, commercial hurdles to clear, things we needed to prove to investors, things I needed to prove to myself. Nonetheless, larger companies had begun to find our clinical data compelling, and a few had approached us to discuss potential partnerships. I had been hesitant at first but thought that working with an already established sales force would be the fastest way to get the device to patients who needed it the most. And now, there it was in black and white. Boston Scientific, one of the largest and most innovative health care companies in the world, wanted to buy my company for $275 million. Commence sliding onto the floor.

A few long moments passed before I finally collected myself enough to climb to my knees and scrutinize the deal memo Rakesh had forwarded. I read the whole thing over five times looking for the "gotcha!" but I couldn't find one. It looked like a fair deal. I sat in stunned silence. I printed out the email attachment—as if holding the piece of paper would make the whole thing seem more real.

I only wanted one thing at that time, to be with my best friend and husband, Rajeev, who was at his office in the SoMa district of San Francisco, about a fifteen-minute drive away. Surely, sharing this moment with Raj would shake me out of my disbelief, I thought as I ran down three flights of stairs, barely remembering my shoes and entirely forgetting my jacket. When I arrived at Raj's office, I double-parked and called him urgently. He was CEO of a growing tech startup, which meant we were both putting in long days and rarely interrupted each other during work hours. I rushed, "Hey, babe, come to the front of your office, I have news. And maybe pack your shit for the day."

"Uh . . . hey?" Raj replied, surprised. "Why are you at my office? I have a day full of meetings, I can't just disappear. I'm not packing up my stuff."

Finally, he agreed to come down and say a quick hello. I got out of the car and waited on the sidewalk. When he arrived, I pulled him close and whispered the news in his ear, before showing him the paper that contained the deal terms. He read it a couple of times, running a hand through his dark hair, chuckling quietly, the way he does when he can't quite grasp what he's seeing. He put a hand on my cheek and smiled. "Okay, let me go grab my shit."

When Raj returned, he declared champagne was in order, suggesting we go to the Ritz-Carlton in Half Moon Bay, about a half hour away. Driving south along the coastal highway, the two of us sat mostly in silence, taking in the views of steep green cliffs with pounding ocean waves below, a stark contrast to the towering high-rises of the financial district in the city I loved. San Francisco is a city of contradictions, loaded with tech startups and some of the world's wealthiest people, yet also with vast homeless encampments. But for all its problems, the Bay Area is still the place that had readily welcomed my brown, immigrant parents when they arrived from India in the 1970s, and to me it would always be home. In a way, it was easier to get lost in the view than to absorb my current reality—the news of the deal, the validation of the effort, the changes the accomplishment would bring still too fresh to process.

When I was only eighteen years old, a first-year student at UC Berkeley, I met Raj. He was a senior, studying economics and computer science and playing Metallica on his guitar. From the beginning, he made time and space for me and my dreams. A few dates in, while eating burgers at a Fuddruckers near campus (he avoided onions to be polite; I did not), I told him about my plans. In part due to my own medical experiences, I would one day start a company dedicated to women's health. He didn't bat his (particularly long) eyelashes. He thought that my desire to have such an impact was cool and that I should "totally go for it." Years later, he would tell me that hearing about my entrepreneurial aspirations further inspired him to start his own company. He asked if my health problem would come back again, and when I said I didn't know, he said, "Well, I'll be here if it does."

In Raj, I found someone who, starting from the earliest days of my adventure, supported me fully. When we got married in 2011, we began life as a couple focused on building our individual careers. Raj had previously thought he wanted to stay at home and raise kids but instead embarked upon a challenging tech career in marketing and product development. I, in the meantime, fixated on launching my company. My twenties were marked by a series of long nights working, the company of my laptop often replacing the company of friends and family. I put a waterproof whiteboard in the shower stall, using it to map out solutions to the latest problem my fledgling business was facing. Raj and I would talk about both of our companies late into each evening. Once he fell asleep, I would work until 3:00 or 4:00 a.m., quietly typing so that the noise of the keyboard wouldn't wake him. Later, I pushed myself through more than fifty rejections when trying to raise our first round of funding, missed close friends' weddings while running a big clinical study, taken a board call from my hospital bed in the maternity ward, and spent much of the year before the sale navigating tough acquisition negotiations while nursing a baby. Raj supported me through all of this. Now, as we approached the gates of the Ritz, I took a deep breath. *Had it all been worth it?*

Nothing seemed real. Would an idea I had been dreaming about for nearly two decades have the resources behind it to reach patients? Could I now better support my recently divorced mother? Maybe even do something extravagant to thank her for the last ten months she had been living with us and helping raise our son? Could Raj and I take a vacation in style? Would my early investors and first employees finally be rewarded for taking a risk on me?

As I took in my surroundings, a familiar feeling washed over me, one of not belonging. Followed by another familiar feeling, self-doubt. I wondered if my good fortune would suddenly evaporate. After all, this was just an initial letter of intent, not the full contract. In some sense, it was just the start of a long negotiation process that could still go off the rails.

Somewhere in the middle of my second glass of champagne, the sunlight pouring through the windows warming me, I started to relax. A knot years in the making, a tension in my chest, began to loosen its grip. As we made our way home that evening, rushing to get back in time for our bedtime routine with our son— wrestling him into the bath, making silly faces in the mirror afterward, singing him to sleep—it almost felt as if nothing had changed.

But everything had. What that piece of paper represented was vindication—I'm a (relatively) young, (very) quirky brown woman who never went to business or medical school and grew up in a house where Hindi was spoken as often as English. I had been underrated and doubted my entire life. That sheet of paper relieved the mega-weight of having to prove myself more than others might have to, a weight that I had been carrying for years. Raj carried this burden with me, and our relief was expressed in that day's quiet but extravagant (for us, who were rather frugal) celebration. In this moment, I realized that the single most important decision I made in my career was to push forward even while being doubted by so many. Doubted by the famous inventor who fell asleep while I was speaking to him. Doubted by the venture capitalists who started chatting with one another as if I weren't there when I was in the middle of pitching them for money. Doubted by the engineers who, after saying they would work with me, simply stopped picking up my calls. Doubted by the guy who came to my booth during a trade show, looked over my shoulder, and asked to speak with the CEO of the company. Doubted by family and "friends." Underrated by many. Doubted even by myself.

The morning after the champagne celebration, my mom, Rajeev, and I, all still in our pajamas, gathered around the kitchen table. Our son Shreyas, now a toddler, balanced on my left hip as I held a pen in my right hand. In front of me lay the signature page of the deal memo. By this time, I'd consulted my core staff and my board members. I'd also lain awake half the night, wondering whether selling the company would feel like selling a piece of my own heart. And yet in that moment, surrounded by

the most important people in my life, all the fears I'd been holding on to—that I didn't deserve this sort of success, that it wasn't
fully earned, or could be suddenly taken away—were replaced
by calmness and unbridled joy. I pressed my hand to the page
and signed my name.

I wrote this book for people like me, for those who feel underrated, the weight of doubt pulling at us while we try to reach
our goals. I don't have complete answers and quick remedies to
offer, most especially when it comes to combating entrenched
bigotry, unconscious bias, or the insipid but widespread practice
of merely overlooking people who are somehow "different."
There are no easy answers. There is no simple formula. But my
own route, I realize, involved climbing a certain ladder, one less
talked about than the traditional ladder to success.

Maybe you've been underrated because you were born a
certain color or gender, or into a certain socioeconomic class, or
because you have unconventional ideas. Even those born with
certain privileges can feel underrated. One of my white male
colleagues once told me he was simply too short to succeed in
the business world. Maybe you've been passed over when being
considered for a promotion, or when trying to voice your opinion
in a meeting, by overly competitive classmates or a dismissive
professor. Underrated by people of other races who don't see
you as belonging, underrated by those in your own race for not
belonging quite enough, held down by stereotypes and expectations, made into a caricature.

I hope my experiences and the insights I've learned will show
you that the very qualities that put you on the outside with certain people or in certain environments are, in fact, your strengths.

That your power lies in being able to recognize those qualities, define them, and leverage them in pursuit of your dreams. We'll talk about dreams in these pages, because I've learned that for me, I'm more likely to be successful when my work is attached to a wholly felt passion. It keeps me going when things get tough, and they will get tough. And knowing your passion comes from knowing your story, even if—maybe especially if—that story is one that others have doubted.

We'll investigate self-sabotaging thoughts, finding and strengthening a network of true believers, why seemingly preposterous ideas have merit, raising not just money but money that comes with conviction attached, and attracting the right talent and knowing when it's time stop underrating—and start re-rating—yourself. More than anything, I want to help you build your own ladder—and scale it. The first time in your life someone underrated you? The casual disregard they or others have expressed toward your talent, or life experience, or drive? Well, that's nothing but rocket fuel that, harnessed the right way, can propel you forward. I know this for a fact, because it's what got me to where I am now.

And to understand where my journey from being underrated to unbeatable began, we have to go back to an earlier, more painful trip to the floor.

A Good Indignation

Finding a Problem You Want to Work On

"A good indignation brings out all one's powers."
—RALPH WALDO EMERSON

When the emergency room doctor asked me if I was pregnant, I snorted, "Not unless it was an immaculate conception." Even in skewering pain, I was a smartass thirteen-year-old. I spent the start of my freshman year of high school studying, thinking about boys (but not sleeping with them), and playing basketball, often showing up to class soiled with mud from dribbling a ball between classrooms. The physician, incredulous at my declaration of abstinence, ordered a pregnancy test among many others anyway. I stared at the sterile white hospital walls, trying to get comfortable on a plank-like emergency room bed, wondering how I'd gotten there on a Tuesday evening.

An hour before, I'd been in my bedroom, writing an English

paper on Ralph Waldo Emerson. I had the window open to let in a breeze that carried the scent of the oak trees surrounding my family's home in Saratoga, a small town tucked away at the base of the Santa Cruz Mountains, an hour south of San Francisco. I was sitting at my desk with my legs kicked up on my bed when I felt a burst of pain, a firework exploding in my abdomen. There was no lead-up, no warning, just severe and sudden stabbing. I looked down, half expecting to find an open wound. I felt light-headed, on the verge of fainting.

I forced myself to put one foot in front of the other and make my way from my bedroom to the kitchen, as the hallway started to spin. My mom was preparing one of her delicious Indian meals, rich with cumin, coriander, and garlic—the scent of which would draw hungry neighbors to our front door, hoping she'd invite them in. That day, she stood at the sink with her back toward me, facing the window to the front yard. I took a deep breath and managed to whisper one of the most powerful words in any language—"Mom"—before passing out, crashing to the floor.

When I woke, I was stretched out in the backseat of our car, with my mom driving at a high speed. How did she get me into the car? My dad had been at work, my eleven-year-old sister out with a friend. My mom is barely 5 foot 3 inches, and I was already taller than her. Maybe it was residual strength left over from being on her college swim team. More likely, it was just the force of her love.

At the hospital, a nurse put me in a wheelchair and rushed us into the ER, leaving us to wait in what felt like an all-white cubby. I tried to stand up straight, and passed out again, my mom catching me before I hit the floor. Coming to, I realized the trick to not passing out was to stay hunched over, as if compressing my still-invisible wound.

Eventually, the ER physician walked in, felt my abdomen, and started asking me questions. Are you sexually active? (Ugh, come on, man, in front of my mom?) Did you eat something old? He thought I was either pregnant or more likely had appendicitis, and instructed me to get into a hospital gown and await the arrival of a surgeon.

The pregnancy test was unsurprisingly negative, and the surgeon concluded it wasn't appendicitis, but he wasn't sure what it was. He suggested I take Tylenol to address the searing pain that had not let up since I'd arrived and arranged for me to get an ultrasound the next day, as it was now late and their ultrasound technician had left hours earlier.

As we headed home, I was scared and confused, feeling I had no control over my body, and the Tylenol didn't do much to dull the physical pain. That night, my mom slept next to me on my bedroom floor, my sister checking on us periodically. Listening to my mom breathe helped me control my fear. As exhausted as I was, I didn't get any sleep, and now that I am a mother myself, I realize she didn't either.

The next day, we finally got an answer to what was wrong: I had a complex ovarian cyst. Complex because it was part solid, part water. Complex because it might be cancer.

Why me? ran through my head.

I knew that whatever was happening with my body was going to make me feel even more out of step with the normal swirl of high school life than I already did. I had a few close friends and attentive teachers, but like most kids my age, I was still insecure

about who I was and how people felt about me. In general, I'd
grown accustomed to feeling pretty different, a little outside of
any group I was in. Somehow my body always seemed to contribute to these issues—like how I was accident-prone. One of
my earliest memories was when my sister, Swasti, was born. I was
two and a half years old, and I was so excited to meet her that
I tripped while running down the hospital corridor, falling onto
the floor and sending my two front teeth flying into the air.

As if going into kindergarten with a broken elbow, being
forced to stay at my desk watching the other kids play during
recess wasn't enough, my unconventional hobbies and interests
didn't make elementary school any easier. I would eagerly wait
for the bell to ring for recess. As soon as it did, I would bolt out
of my chair and run out the door to the school's grassy field, past
the other girls, who would find a large patch of small flowers and
tie the stems together to create necklaces. I went to the edge of
the field, where the chain-link fence met the dirt, where weeds
would grow. I would kneel in the earth, overturning leaves and
large rocks, hunting for insects. I still remember the thrill of un-
covering a beetle with an iridescent blue coating, or watching pill
bugs with legs that move so fast that one might think that they
glide instead of walk. And ladybugs—with beautifully imperfect
black dots on a bright red shell, a gift of God's paintbrush, the
symmetry of the wings underneath, a most perfect work of evo-
lution. I would collect them, making sure not to hurt them. Then
I would take notes on their habits, dietary preferences, and mat-
ing cycles. If I found something unique, I would beg the teacher
to let me bring my bug-filled jar to my desk so I could watch them
for a few hours more. It's no wonder the other girls didn't want

to sit with me at lunch, and the boys weren't interested in talking to me either, unless you count the twins who made fun of my large nose. By the time I was in third grade, I already wished I was someone else.

When I was two years old, my family, like many immigrants from India, had moved to the hillside city of Fremont, close to Silicon Valley engineering jobs and affordable housing prices (at the time). My father worked as a software engineer at several tech companies before finally landing at the new internet company Netscape, and I attended a public school called Weibel Elementary nearby. Here a third of my school was made up of Indian American kids like myself, children whose parents had immigrated and who were being raised with one foot in both cultures, Indian and American, so you would think I would fit in. But I seemed to fall into a kind of cultural in-betweenness—no matter how hard I tried to be a part of the group of Indian kids at my school, they weren't interested in playing with me. I was leaving the playground one day when another little Indian girl ran up to me and said, unbidden, "You're not a real Indian." Most of the Indian girls at my school also went to Indian classical or Bollywood dance classes. My mom had at one point encouraged me to try it out but didn't force me, and I had zero interest. I preferred hip-hop class to Kathak class, preferred listening to the soundtrack of *The Lion King* to listening to the latest Bollywood hit. Even though I loved traveling with my mom and sister each summer to my mother's hometown of Chandigarh in the northern state of Punjab, where I played with a large group of cousins and friends; even though *mattar* (peas) slow-cooked with *paneer* (cheese), wrapped up in a soft, freshly made *chapati* (flatbread) tasted like home; even though being Indian was and always will be a big part of my identity, I was left out.

Unable to fit in with the Indian girls, I finally made friends with Rachel. She was from a Chinese American family. Her mom showed me how to make dumplings, my favorite, and how to tell when they are done—not until they float to the top of a boiling pot of water. She'd serve us food and then sit us down on the couch and have us watch videos about Jesus, which did not strike my fourth-grade self as odd. Rachel and I both loved animals, and with our parents, we went to the pet store together to pick out bunnies. I chose the gray one. She picked a white one, though not the one with red eyes as she thought it looked too much like the devil. Soon after, she asked me to join her family's Christian church, saying that otherwise, she couldn't spend time with me anymore. I was already conflicted enough about religion with my mom being a practicing Hindu and my dad an adamant atheist, so I politely declined her offer. It was heartbreaking when every time I tried to sit next to her during lunch after that, she would get up and move.

One friend who was always there for me was Panther, my black Labrador, who I got in fifth grade. He kept me company when other kids wouldn't, placing his head in my lap when he could sense I had had a rough day. But slowly I made human friends, too, and I timidly worked myself into the Indian girls' circle. I agreed to take part in arts and crafts, and tolerated the Bollywood music playing in the background. I enjoyed going to their houses and having regular Saturday playdates. Just as I was starting to feel like I finally had a group of friends, in the summer of 1995, my parents decided that I should go to a private middle school. My parents disagreed on many things, but one thing they were on the same page about is the value of a good education, even if it was at great personal sacrifice to them. So with some additional money from Netscape going public, they could now just afford to send me to one of the best schools in the Bay Area, a small school an hour away in San Jose called the Harker School.

At Harker, teachers were always willing to stay late or give up their lunch breaks to meet with students. The student body, though, provided me with serious culture shock. A larger percentage of the school community was white, and the overall vibe was more progressive than the socially conservative Indian culture I'd been used to in Fremont. I went from not being brown enough to being too brown. In the locker room, I discovered that most of the girls were wearing training bras and shaving their legs. And they discovered with much glee that I was not. When I started wearing a training bra to keep up with them, the Indian girls back in Fremont, whose parents didn't want to rush such things, would make fun of me.

While middle school was marked by jarring change and not fitting in, as I entered high school, I began to find my footing. With internet companies starting to do well in 1998 and 1999, many Bay Area families made money in the dot-com boom, and Harker welcomed many Indian families to their incoming freshman class (several of them from Fremont). Among them, I found friends. I tried out for the basketball team and made it. I enjoyed my first semester of classes. All seemed to be starting to go in the right direction, until that mysterious explosion happened in my abdomen—that thing that might be cancer.

Shortly after the discovery of my ovarian cysts, my mother

brought me to her OB-GYN, Dr. Carole Cooke. She had seen my mom when she was pregnant with me and had held me soon after birth. In contrast to the sterile hospital room and unknown physicians poking and prodding, Dr. Cooke and her office were warm and comforting. She calmly explained the next steps: doctors would do another higher-resolution ultrasound and perform a blood test called CA-125 to try to determine if the mass was cancerous or not. Attempting to provide a silver lining, she noted that ovarian cancer was extremely rare in young women. But I understood that statistics applied to a population and not to an individual, so I found this less reassuring than she had hoped. Why would I assume that I was not going to be part of the 5 percent who did end up with cancer? Statistics are only comforting when you're in the other 95 percent.

Once Dr. Cooke completed the tests she had ordered, all we could do was wait for the results. I obsessed about the fact that I might have cancer. My parents tried to console me with hugs and encouragement, but what I craved was some control, or at least a sense of control.

Until this point in my life, I had always trusted my doctors and felt safe in their hands, whether they were mending a broken elbow or dealing with my chronic sinus infections. I thought medicine had all the answers and had no reason to doubt any of the tools being used. As I read about how ovarian cancer was diagnosed, though, I started to doubt my confidence. To ease my mind, I wanted to learn as much as I could about what I was facing. I had been long fascinated by scientific inquiry, observing what is naturally occurring and coming up with hypotheses to explain it. Remember the bugs? I was steadfastly filling scientific notebooks about how changes in insects' food and habitat impacted their behavior. (I also did this with frogs in a neighbor's pond, sneaking into their backyard while they were at work. This resulted in a less than pleasant call to my parents and the neighbors ultimately draining the pond with tadpoles still in it, which gave me nightmares for years.)

I locked myself in my bedroom and bent over my laptop, putting different terms into Yahoo! (Google was only starting to emerge into mainstream use back then)—beginning with "ovarian cyst" and "ovarian cancer." I learned that ovarian cysts are common and generally harmless, and that they occur every month as part of a woman's reproductive cycle and usually dissolve on their own. Only in some instances does the patient even know she has a cyst, as most of them don't cause any pain or discomfort. The problem is that if there is a cyst, it is difficult to know whether or not it is cancerous. Ultrasound, I discovered, was the primary means of detecting ovarian cysts and it only provided a black-and-white image of the mass—telling the physician that a mass is present, but not always if it is benign or malignant. Cysts can either be entirely fluid filled, completely solid, or complex (a mix of both). Fluid-filled cysts are benign, but the other two might be cancerous, or they might not be—an ultrasound can't tell. Then I searched for the blood test that Dr. Cooke mentioned, which would check for something known as CA-125.

By the time I had my own health scare, I had started to understand the concepts behind scientific theory (I'm glad I kept on "playing" with those bugs despite what the other kids said). As I read more about it, something didn't add up. The blood test looks for cancer antigen 125, which is a protein found in the bloodstream, and while it is good at finding it, having an elevated level of this protein doesn't necessarily mean that you have cancer. The problem is that CA-125 levels in a woman's body fluctuate and could be elevated by something as simple as menstruation or other benign conditions. Ultimately, this test is accurate only 50 percent of the time—no better than a coin toss.

A week later, we were back in Dr. Cooke's office to review results of both the high-resolution ultrasound and CA-125 test. The new ultrasound confirmed the previous one—there was a mass, and it was complex. And my CA-125 was indeed elevated.

Our family was now faced with a daunting choice. Either I would undergo an invasive exploratory surgery to visualize the ovary and surrounding anatomy to determine if I had cancer, or we'd wait to see if the mass grew, or—put another way—if the cancer developed further. Doing a biopsy of a cyst isn't recommended because if it is cancerous, malignant cells may spill into the rest of the body. Because of this, and because of the way cysts sometimes fuse to ovaries, the ovary itself is often removed when doctors attempt to remove a cyst. Even if we did just the exploratory surgery, there was a risk of scarring or damaging my ovary, which could potentially impact my chances of getting pregnant or cause lifelong hormonal imbalance. Waiting was also risky, since ovarian cancers tend to be aggressive. A patient's odds of surviving five years drops from 95 percent to about 50 percent if the cancer spreads from its initial location.

Still, we decided not to rush the decision. As the pain subsided into a dull ache, I pushed myself to go back to school, wanting a sense of normalcy. But I had trouble concentrating during class, constantly replaying the conversation with Dr. Cooke and focusing on what bad news might come my way. I would often look past my friends while they were talking to me, preoccupied. I could tell that my teachers were tracking both my academics and my mood carefully, having been informed by my parents about what was happening. One day during human anatomy, normally one of my favorite classes, the teacher called on me to answer a question about the immune system. I had tuned out early in the lesson and now found myself staring at her wide-eyed, a blank expression on my face. I was lost. Ms. Anita Chetty was stern, with high expectations; she was the last teacher you wanted to ire. When she asked me to come see her after school, I knew I was in trouble.

Walking into her classroom at the end of the day, I was surprised to find a 3-D model of the female reproductive system on display. As she sat down in front of me, I readied myself for a lecture. Instead, with a slight softening of her expression, she asked, "Do you want to learn more about the biology behind your condition?" When I nodded mutely, she continued. "There," she said as she pointed, "you have two ovaries. They sit above your uterus, and are connected to your uterus by the fallopian tubes. They contain unfertilized eggs, and help control your hormone levels." At home, my family had little interest in talking about the female reproductive system. It was just too uncomfortable, so we'd basically taken to referencing my illness only glancingly and avoiding words like *uterus* and *ovary*. Even though I had read some of this online, it was comforting to go through it with Ms. Chetty. I had spent a month now feeling stressed and scared, but her forthrightness calmed me down.

Hungry for more information, I went to the public library

and ended up searching the stacks for medical journals that could explain my condition in more detail. That was the first time I held such a book in my hands. And from the limited number of articles on ovarian cysts and cancer, I realized that the scientific community had a limited understanding of ovarian cancer. Compared to other conditions, there was less research available, meaning there would be no easy, clear answers. My family and I would need to decide more on gut instinct than medical knowledge, which is what we did. One evening, after my sister excused herself from the dinner table, I told my parents that I agreed with them—I wanted to skip the surgery, and wait to see what happened. They were supportive of the decision, and Dr. Cooke was as well.

After six months, the cyst dissolved on its own in a painful burst, which happened in the middle of Spanish class and caused me to pass out. We finally knew that it wasn't cancer. My family was able to relax again, and I was, too, but as my fear faded, a new emotion took its place. I was angry. We'd had to do too much guessing and waiting. We were forced to make so many impossible choices.

For the next two years, the pain came and went: a cyst would bloom in my abdomen and then disappear, taking me out of school for days. Sometimes it would cause a dull ache; other times the pain would be acute and surprising, like a sucker punch to the gut. I felt so nauseated in the mornings that even when I did make it to school, I was almost always late, setting a frenzied pace for the rest of the day. I couldn't do standard stuff like wearing a backpack—carrying heavy things apparently increased the risk of causing more cysts. I was so fatigued that I eventually had to quit the basketball team, one of my only remaining anchors to a normal high school experience. My grades started to slip, reflecting my ups and downs: I sometimes got Cs on my report card, other semesters I made the honor roll. High school was hard enough without the story of my health crisis circulating around the hallways. I remember a boy running up to me and saying, "Surbhi, I heard your entire ovary burst! So gross " I tried to explain, "Actually, it was just an attached cyst . . . never mind."

Ms. Chetty's classroom became a sort of refuge for me. The two of us would talk about my condition at the end of the day as my peers rushed out to after-school hangouts and debate clubs. Sometimes we'd run science experiments, just to get my mind off things. She noticed I was especially interested in her lecture on neurology, so she ordered different species for me to conduct brain dissections on, like a snake or a cat. When I was less than enthusiastic about it, informing her that I preferred to interact with live animals versus dead ones, she came up with another idea: What if we started a saltwater tank?

For the next several months, I spent my spare time learning about the right pH levels and temperature required for different types of fish, delighted by the colors of the Australian red-and-white coral banded shrimp we'd picked out (and was horrified when the anemone in the tank ate it). As we watched the fish, she would listen patiently to me prattle on about my crushes and offer advice. One time she got distracted while cleaning the tank with a suction tube and ended up drenching her entire face in dirty saltwater—only to laugh at herself. Who would have thought? Ms. Chetty, known for being one of the most intimidating and toughest teachers in our school, was also deeply attentive, caring, and funny.

I didn't fully realize it at the time, but Ms. Chetty, as well as my English teacher Ms. Sharron Mittelstet, were quietly and patiently channeling my anger into knowledge, feeding my curiosity, and gently steering me toward the realization that what I was going through had significance and value. Ms. Chetty helped me learn about my condition and develop my scientific mind. Ms. Mittelstet taught me that writing about the complicated emotions I was cycling through could help me deal with them. She spent her lunch breaks and many after-school hours reading my writing, helping me refine my thoughts and identify my feelings. When it came time to apply to college, I had my heart set on going to the University of California at Berkeley, since it was close to home and had a stellar biology program. Ms. Mittelstet coached me through crafting a personal statement that spelled out a dream that, thanks to her and Ms. Chetty, was taking shape in my young mind: I wanted to further my education so that I could someday start a company focused on women's health. I wanted to find solutions to the problems I'd faced personally, and help others avoid some of the uncertainty and pain I'd felt.

Berkeley admitted only 15 percent of those who applied. Although the school required an essay, the weight of admissions decisions at that time was based largely on a student's SAT scores and grades. Given the disruption caused by my illness and the uneven grades that resulted, I knew that getting in would be a long shot. I was so scared and stressed out that I developed a temporary twitch in my left eye, and the insomnia I'd had since I was a kid worsened. I put all my energy into my personal statement, since it provided a voice that my grades and test scores couldn't. That piece, along with my heartfelt teacher references, was strong enough to catch the attention of an admissions officer who decided to give me a chance, asking if I'd furnish a doctor's note and more details on how my medical condition had impacted my grades. I was accepted. I felt both grateful and lucky, and more driven than ever. My high school teachers had helped me not only fight through a disadvantage but to see that disadvantage as an opportunity to find my passion and motivation.

At Berkeley, I dedicated myself to learning more about women's health, studying the foundations of molecular and cell biology, and taking courses in women's studies. I got a work-study job in bioengineering research with a professor who was trying to grow livers in a lab using stem cells, helping decrease the long wait list for livers in the United States. Growing organs! I loved how challenging it was not only to learn about complex scientific pathways but also to be creative at the same time. The work was fascinating, and I was motivated by the fact that it could benefit so many patients in the long run. All the while, I fought feelings of inadequacy, aware that I had just barely made it into such a prestigious university, and wondering if I deserved to be there. I didn't know that there was a name for this at the time— impostor syndrome—but I did my best to push past those feelings and make the most of the opportunities I had.

My struggle with ovarian cysts, which ended after the hormone fluctuations that come with puberty, had given me a glimpse of something much bigger than myself—a chasm of inequity, a specific and identifiable problem in the medical field. My fear and frustrations as a teenage patient dealing with a gynecological condition for which there was no remedy were part of a larger landscape in which women were often subject to lengthy diagnostic times or solutions from the early 1900s. The more I learned, the more my indignation grew. I became aware, for example, that female patients hadn't even been included in clinical trials for life-saving drugs until the 1970s, because they were considered too dainty. This meant that many medications had dosage recommendations optimized for men. In fact, there could be more effective medications out there for women, but we would never know. When it came to ovarian cancer, I learned that each year, 300,000 women in the US had their ovaries removed, though according to the Centers for Disease Control and Prevention (CDC), only 21,000 women were ultimately diagnosed with ovarian cancer, making it a life-altering but often unnecessary surgery. Even so, only 20 percent of ovarian cancer cases were caught at an early stage.

Other serious conditions that impact women receive little attention from medical research or the development of effective treatments. To this day, endometriosis, a painful disease impacting four million women in the US, takes anywhere from four to eleven years to diagnose. More than one uterus a minute is removed in the US, a major surgery done unnecessarily. And one of the leading causes of infertility in women is fallopian tube blockage, which is currently diagnosed by a medical procedure known as hysterosalpingography (HSG) that is painful and inaccurate—but hasn't been replaced for more than one hundred years. The evidence is everywhere. Women have so long been thought of as second class, and it has yielded something we don't deserve and are suffering under: a second-class medical system.

This is when a dream started to take shape for me. It began in high school, grew in college, and drove me through the years that followed: I wanted to spend my life improving the quality of care women receive, by replacing antiquated approaches with cutting-edge innovation, providing them the standard of health care they deserve. It would start with finding a better way to detect ovarian cancer.

2

Building Your Own Ladder

Gaining the Right Experience

I went to college with my grand plan of starting a company in women's health, and yet I had no idea how to make that happen. I knew perhaps what to study, but what should I do for work?

So, when the time came to apply for summer internships, I relied on being practical and looked for a "good job" in a "good field." Unsure if it would be best to get experience in the business world or technical and scientific world, my search was wide and included investment banks, pharmaceutical companies, and medical device manufacturers.

A couple of banks offered me interviews that, if everything went well, would segue to full-time positions upon graduation. But I felt uneasy when a managing director at one bank asked me how I would price a new pharmaceutical drug. I focused on patient need and wasn't interested in talking about maximizing profit margins. After sitting through more interviews, seeing various corporate cultures, and learning about the kind of work I would be doing at each place, I realized that starting with the technical, scientific path—the kind of work I'd enjoyed since experimenting on my own as a kid—was right for me. I took an internship at Abbott Vascular, a Santa Clara company that manufactures an array of medical devices used by cardiologists and surgeons to address heart problems. I would get to apply the theory I was learning at school and be able to work on what interested me, but for half the salary of what an investment bank or consultancy would pay.

At the age of twenty-one, I was not uninterested in making money. I wanted to feel financially stable enough to help support my mom if I had to, as my parents' marriage was rocky. Plus, I had friends who made enough money in a single summer to frequent the Michelin-starred restaurants of San Francisco on a weekly basis. But I learned that what really mattered for my first job wasn't the money: it was gaining the right experience. This is what I've seen with other entrepreneurs, too—even if they end up on the business end, including running a startup, they often begin on a technical path so they can learn the skills needed to actually create the product. If you want to create a jewelry brand, for example, learn how to make jewelry ahead of founding a small business, like Christine Guibara and Prerna Sethi, who both started making their own jewelry and thinking of designs before launching their own companies. If you want to be part of bringing the next big app to the public, take courses in coding or teach yourself, so that even if you are not doing the actual coding in the long run, you know what the people who code are doing, and you have the experience to ask the right questions and judge the results. Kevin Systrom, cofounder of Instagram, one of the most used apps in the world, was obsessed with photography and wanted to find a way to make it easy to share images on social media. He also started to learn coding when he was in middle school and continued learning into adulthood.

In the late 1950s, Silicon Valley's first three IPOs were companies that were founded and run by scientists and engineers: Varian was founded by Stanford engineering professors including Edward Leonard Ginzton, a Ukrainian American engineer. Hewlett Packard was founded by two Stanford engineering graduate students, Bill Hewlett and David Packard. Ampex was founded by a Russian-born American mechanical/electrical engineer, Alexander Poniatoff. More recently, DoorDash, Airbnb, and Instacart all had engineers as cofounders.

Business skills can be acquired while you're building your company. But mastering the technical skills needed to execute the business you want to be in—whether that's retail, art, health care, organic farming, or green energy—begins with an understanding of that field from a technical perspective.

It's hard to stay focused on gaining the experience you need to get when that sometimes means turning down more money and/or security. The lures of high-paying jobs, of well-trodden paths and systems are hard to ignore—or easy to be seduced by. I've watched so many brilliant minds get sucked into conventional corporate structures and academia. Off went my talented friends, first to law school and then to brand-name law firms, to investment banks where they put in hundred-hour weeks adjusting the font size on someone else's PowerPoint presentation, or to their doctorates and then postdoctorates, chasing the next publication. It seems that the more brilliant you are, the more hardworking, the more people want to put you in their system to climb their ladder—to help them chase their dreams.

When those dreams align with yours, this works. There's nothing wrong with taking a job because you need a job, or with using a job to help you gain the kind of skills you need to facilitate your own long-term dreams. The risk, though, is that as time passes, you forget about your dreams. No one wants to wake up and realize it could be too late in the process, feeling in too deep—too dependent on the money or the structure or the prestige—to find a way out. The higher up you get on someone else's ladder, the harder it is to jump off. Entrepreneurs are people who build their own ladders while also climbing them. It's difficult, sometimes perilous, sometimes disastrous, but in the end, it's your ascent to your dream.

All this said, I am aware that building your own ladder is a privilege and not something everyone can readily do. My dad was born in 1955 to an Indian family in Kenya, which at the time was a British colony. When the British relinquished their control in 1963, people of Indian origin were no longer considered citizens, making it nearly impossible to own land or even get a permit to work. My dad's family moved to Dehradun, India, near the Himalayan foothills, where they joined the burgeoning middle class. In the late 1960s, he was eventually accepted into the Birla Institute of Technology (BITS) in Pilani, one of the very best engineering schools in India.

Frustrated by the political and social challenges in India at the time and intrigued by the potential of a tech revolution and promise of an adventure, my dad immigrated to the US in the mid-1970s alone. He first arrived in New York, like many immigrants before him, and enrolled in Rensselaer Polytechnic Institute and Stony Brook University, earning two master's degrees, one in electrical engineering and another in computer science. He then went to Silicon Valley to work as an entry-level software engineer. Eventually, in 1982, he went back to India, met my mom through their families, and had an arranged marriage. Though she barely knew him, she left her life in India behind to join him in the US.

Money was tight. By the mid-1980s, my father was supporting a young family while also sending funds back to his parents in India. During lunch breaks at his first job, he and his Indian colleagues would find a table in the cafeteria away from their co-workers, hoping to avoid the disdainful looks they got when they opened their *tiffins* full of fragrant food and spicy Indian pickle, *achar*. Buying food from the cafeteria was too costly. Fitting in didn't seem like an option either. While today the CEOs of Microsoft and Google are Indian immigrants, in the early days of Silicon Valley, Indian immigrants, like most immigrants, were often underrated, misunderstood, or feared, and had to work extra hours to prove themselves.

As my father put in long hours at work, my mom did the same at home. She spent her pregnancy with me completely without her family. This was such a stark contrast to what was familiar to her in India, where it's customary for a young mother to live with her extended family and raise children communally.

Pregnant women are pampered by their parents and in-laws. Now, long-distance phone calls home were expensive, and stressful, too: I remember my mom yelling into the telephone receiver, trying to overcome the static and terrible connectivity of international phone lines in the 1980s. Mostly, she had to depend on snail mail to communicate with her parents, even when her father became deathly ill.

My mother is strong and resourceful. When I was a baby in need of diapers, she would look through the newspaper for sales and find the cheapest place to get them. She would then do the calculation on gas, and if the math worked, she would strap me into my car seat and drive an hour in order to save a few dollars. If the sale was good enough, she would hide diapers in the store on random shelves and then direct her friends to find them. Through a series of serendipitous meetings—which sometimes happened at the mailbox—she built close friendships with other young Indian immigrants in the neighborhood. She created her own family, who became my aunties, with whom we spent every weekend. It wasn't just an old-school social network; these women took care of each other, not replacing but supplementing and substituting for the family they left back home.

Eventually, my dad rose to the position of vice president of engineering at a software company. He talked about his dream of starting a company all the time, but he never made the leap. My mom had earned a PhD in Hindi literature in India and had always wanted to teach. She sacrificed a possible opportunity to teach at UC Berkeley to raise my sister and me while supporting my dad's career. Once my sister and I left the house, my mom began teaching Hindi to neighborhood kids, which turned into the first accredited Hindi program in the state of California, and she now lectures at Stanford.

Every choice my parents made along the way had to balance, in their eyes, the risk of building their own ladders with the security offered by existing systems. They always made the safer choices with the aim of supporting my sister and me. Remembering their stories keeps me from being blind to my own privilege. Though plenty of immigrants and plenty of people with kids do start their own companies, and for many, it becomes productive and rewarding, risk tolerance is a personal decision. There isn't a right decision, but as much as possible, let it be *your* decision— not society's or your family's or anyone else's.

So, for my first job, I decided to climb someone else's ladder in order to learn how to build my own. I took on that summer internship at Abbott's offices in Santa Clara, California. The experience taught me about making products, and it turned into a full-time gig; I accepted a position working as an entry-level quality engineer upon graduation. I had considered trying to find a job at a women's health company right out of school, but the field was almost too nascent, receiving less than 5 percent of overall research and development (R&D) funding in the US. Because I was interested in creating medical devices in that same underserved, underrated market, I first wanted to explore the markets where the R&D money was flowing and the innovation was happening, to see what well-resourced work looked like. I was eager to meet people who knew how to create transformational solutions for patients while being in a strictly regulated industry. I hoped it would provide a glimpse of the future I could help build.

All roads seem to track back to the human heart. And mine did literally, because if there was a space in which well-funded innovation was happening, it was cardiology. Almost 50 percent of the US population, about 121.5 million adults, suffer from cardiovascular disease, and 1 in every 5 deaths is from heart disease. The cardiovascular medical device field represents over $50 billion in the US alone. So it's understandable that so much emphasis is given to the industry, and so much money is poured into developing new products that can save and prolong lives.

The company seemed to be making a concerted effort to fill its ranks with more women; Abbott had hired a number of female engineers right out of school that year. As I walked from the elevator to my desk in a sea of cubicles, I would pass by the window-lined offices of upper management, where I noticed a pattern. Most of the big offices housed men. Up until this point, I had studied feminism and women's studies in an academic setting, but this was the first time I *felt* the impact of gender inequality. How would I sit in those offices one day if very few people who looked like me were there now? What was the path? While the female engineers sitting in cubicles around me made me feel hopeful about the future, there was nobody like me atop that ladder, nobody to directly model myself after.

I did, however, love the product I worked on—a catheter that could inject stem cells into the heart to regenerate tissue damaged by a heart attack or other cardiovascular disease. The idea of a catheter was incredible to me. I couldn't believe that you could access almost anywhere in the body by using one, as long as you found the right size and materials to use. Also, my coworkers were fun to be around, and smart. We built a real camaraderie, which is one of the benefits of conventional office life if you happen to fall in with a great group of colleagues. We'd stay late to put the final touches on a patent application and then headed to Molly Magees in Mountain View to have a beer and talk about everything from the latest intra-office drama to debating the most important product specification for the device. I welcomed the company of other women pursuing engineering careers and facing similar challenges to mine.

Because Abbott Vascular was close to my parents' house, I moved back home to save money. Rajeev was living and working in San Francisco, a full hour away, so we saw each other only on weekends.

Unfortunately, the Great Recession was looming in 2008. I survived the first round of layoffs at Abbott, but not the next. Fifteen percent of the company was let go in one swoop. To conserve R&D funds, Abbott suspended work on the catheter, but despite this, I took it personally, sobbing in the parking lot. I wish someone had told me that layoffs happen all the time, even to Steve Jobs, Oprah Winfrey, Walt Disney, and Thomas Edison.

Soon after, Abbott offered me a position to oversee the quality of the packaging of its medical devices. But I knew that dedicating myself to ensuring that labels were properly adhered to boxes would take me one step further away from my ultimate goal of getting R&D experience and starting a company. As I considered this option, I cold-contacted a medical device startup that was developing a catheter-like device that would inject stem cells into the heart. It was similar to the catheter I had worked on for Abbott Vascular, and I explained my experience and how I believed in the promise of this type of product and was hungry to continue that kind of work. To my surprise, I scored an interview with Dave Snow, head of R&D of the then fifteen-person cardiovascular company.

I was nervous, interviewing for an engineering position without a formal engineering degree or product design experience. At Abbott, I had worked as a quality engineer, where a degree in a scientific discipline is adequate because you're not actually designing products but crafting and executing testing to ensure overall compliance and quality of the product. The position at this startup would be a transition to designing the product itself, and a degree in engineering was usually required.

For the interview, I drove to their office in South San Francisco, a mostly industrial city neighboring San Francisco. When I arrived and entered through the front door, which led directly into a dark hallway, I couldn't help but note how different it was from Abbott's grand lobby and waiting room. I excitedly chuckled to myself, "Startup life."

The receptionist took me to a poorly lit conference room, where my nerves really kicked in. I realized how much I really wanted this job. How could I prove that I was capable of learning complex engineering principles, and that despite the fact my degree was in molecular and cell biology, I thought like an engineer? Because I did!

Finally, Dave Snow, my would-be boss, walked into the room. In his mid-forties, with sky-blue eyes and blond hair, he was soft-spoken and direct in his questioning. His confident but kind demeanor immediately put me at ease. He described the job as being R&D related but also mentioned that there was opportunity to help improve their quality systems. Dave posed the same question I'd been asked when interviewing at Abbott: Where do you see yourself in five years? My answer hadn't changed: ultimately, I would start a company in women's health. For now, I wanted to learn, grow, and contribute to the work being done at a startup. Though we hit it off right away and I could tell that he thought my work at Abbott was relevant, Dave's body language seemed to show he was hesitant.

When I got home, I described the whole thing to Rajeev—the office, the job, the thoughtful person I'd be working for—feeling like I'd found my perfect stepping stone. So, when Dave called me later that week, rejecting me for the position, I was despondent. I didn't want to let the opportunity go. I had to find a way in.

A few days after Dave's initial rejection, my mind flicked back to the interview. I recalled he had mentioned something about quality control. I called him and proposed that instead of giving me a full-time salaried position, we could both test the waters with a consulting job, which would allow me to help them with quality-related items and demonstrate my abilities as an engineer. I knew this was a risky move; the economy hadn't yet stabilized, and I had just been laid off from my previous job. Didn't I want some security? Was I even any good if I got laid off so quickly? Dave was open to discussing a consulting position but couldn't promise me a set number of hours.

Ultimately, I had three options to choose from for my next step: continue to search for another opportunity, take the full-time, more secure offer from Abbott Vascular, or gamble a little and learn a lot by accepting a part-time, short-term R&D consulting role at this startup. I chose the startup because it was the most aligned with my ultimate goal. I had to move past my own self-doubt that the role wouldn't turn into something more permanent by recalling how much I wanted to start a company dedicated to women's health, and the risks I was willing to take to get there. And while I didn't know if I was good enough to hang on to a job, especially an engineering one, I was going to try. In this moment, my good indignation overpowered my self-doubt. I started the part-time gig in September 2009. This was the first — but not the last — time Dave would take a big risk on me.

On my first day of work, Dave took me out for a welcome lunch to a little hole-in-the-wall Vietnamese restaurant. Over our steaming bowls of *pho*, I learned that his favorite noodle soup is Malaysian *laksa*, which he enjoyed during his extensive travels in Southeast Asia. Boston bred and Boston proud, he had spent time living in Australia to expand his view of the world. He was an avid skier and mountain climber, though he gave up the latter after the birth of his daughter. He mentioned, too, that he had come up with a plan for teaching me the engineering skills I needed to be successful. He offered to provide reading he thought was helpful and said he would be happy to spend extra time teaching me mechanical engineering concepts as needed.

Dave made himself available to teach me what I needed to know and gave me a book about medical device research and development so I could better understand some important engineering principles that impact design. Over my first weeks on the job, he patiently answered questions, and as I continued to develop my knowledge, he assigned me more challenging tasks.

After I'd been at the startup for about two months, the

company made me a full-time offer as a product development engineer, a position in their R&D group, working under Dave. About six months into the full-time position, I had a performance review. A deluge of insecure thoughts started to take over—entry level, no engineering degree—was I doing a good job? But Dave didn't share any negative feedback and said he appreciated the fact that I wasn't afraid to take on anything, even if I hadn't done it before. I was happy that I hadn't let him down.

My relationship with Dave continued to grow. I admired his commitment to being a family man. He worked hard but still managed to spend time with his kids in the evening, and never missed a doctor's appointment—something I didn't fully appreciate the difficulty of until later. I often saw roses or other gifts sitting on his desk that he was bringing home for his wife, Velvet. I bought a toy car to keep at my desk so that I could play with Dave's kids whenever they came to the office. Dave took his mentorship of me seriously, continuing to furnish me with professional learning opportunities while also getting to know me as a person. Once, after I mentioned wanting to find a drivable weekend trip to take with Rajeev, Dave left a newspaper clipping describing Ashland, Oregon, and the Shakespeare festival on my desk.

I also loved the startup atmosphere—the collaboration, the energy. I didn't miss the more regular hours of Abbott. Even though we had often stayed late, it was nothing like what I was putting in at the startup. I was okay giving up Abbott's premium benefits, its basketball courts and on-campus cafeteria, and other perks.

Before I had the guarantee of a full-time offer, for practicality,

I continued to interview for other jobs. The one that ended up mattering most was with Roy Chin, CEO of a medical device company called SpineView. Born in China, he was sharp and spoke his mind no matter how controversial the subject. His office was gargantuan, and he had a desk to match. I felt tiny, tucked into the back corner, intimidated and impressed by his success.

Examining my résumé, Roy asked me what I wanted to do in ten years. I gave him the same answer I had given everyone else: I wanted to start a medical device company dedicated to women's health. I told him that I'd always figured I would need experience before being able to start something of my own.

Even with this twenty-two-year-old inexperienced woman sitting in front of him, Roy didn't hesitate. He said that I would absolutely be able to start a company before I turned thirty. I didn't believe him. He gave me what turned out to be invaluable advice, explaining that a company only consists of so many parts, and in medical devices, the main parts are R&D, preclinical (testing done in a lab), clinical trials, manufacturing, reimbursement, marketing, and sales. All I needed to do was get a good understanding of each of those areas, and then I would be off to the races.

Despite his encouragement, the interview wasn't a success in the traditional sense. I wasn't offered a job. But it was one of the most meaningful turns of my life because I heard what he said to me and was able to climb my own ladder faster using his insight and advice. It also emphasized the concept of showing up and listening to what experienced people have to say. Someone like Roy isn't under any obligation to offer advice, but he did, and I left the conversation armed with a new belief:

my goal should be starting this company as soon as I felt like I was able to, instead of waiting for a certain number of years of experience. Roy also told me that I would be able to sleep and spend time with my family while running a company. (I'm still figuring out that part.)

I had positive examples of management and leadership in Dave and in Roy, but sometimes I learned just as much by observing behaviors I thought would not work for me personally as a leader. For example, I thought the CEO of the startup I worked for was too wishy-washy in his decision-making, at least for my taste. Our team would work nights and weekends to hit a deadline, only to find out two weeks later that the effort was no longer a priority. To me, the frustration inside upper management was palpable and sometimes created a tense atmosphere. I tucked away a lesson in setting consistent goals, both short-term and long-term, for my team and offering explanations for when those goals did have to change.

My immediate goal was to keep my head down and continue learning. Following Roy Chin's advice about gaining experience in as many arenas inside the company as possible, I made sure I finished all of my main assignments on time, and then would switch to other tasks, taking on small projects and collaborating with people in different departments. As a result, I was able to go into the clean room (a sterile room where people wear what look like space suits) and understand the importance of manufacturing devices in a way that scales. I learned the right way to hold a blade while cutting tubing for a catheter. I was exposed to clinical study design as well as the product development life cycle.

I worked hard enough that at one point the VP of operations, Andy, took notice. He approached me about taking a full-time role as a manager in the quality department. This could potentially be life-changing because I'd be taking an early leap into management and doubling my salary. I had spent some time with Andy and liked learning from him. I was flattered by the proposal. But I also kept my ultimate dream in mind, and I didn't think that being a manager in the quality department would bring me any closer to having the technical tools I needed to start my own company, even though I knew I would have to manage a team one day. I felt continuing to do a deep dive into R&D was more immediately important, so I turned down the job and its higher salary in favor of staying in R&D with Dave.

Even as I felt like I was flourishing in my job, my personal life was growing unexpectedly hectic. My beloved dog, Panther, was diagnosed with cancer and dying, so I administered pain meds to him and sat by him for hours on the floor of our garage, his constant vomiting and diarrhea making it impossible to keep him in the house. My mom's oldest brother passed away, and not too long after that, my grandmother was diagnosed with breast cancer, leaving my mother distressed. Rajeev and I were planning our wedding in Half Moon Bay, which would involve relatives flying in from India and more logistics and opinions than I could handle. It was going to be a big fat Indian wedding over three days—a *mehndi* ceremony on Thursday during which I would have my hands and feet coated in henna, a *sangeet* on Friday where our friends and families would put on choreographed dances for us, and then finally, the wedding and reception on Saturday. While being excited about my own wedding, I worried constantly about my mother, whose marriage to my father continued to suffer as she flew back and forth to India trying to care for her own mom.

My grandmother died in the winter of 2011, just five months before Rajeev and I exchanged our vows. While she was at the hospital for one of her frequent visits. an infection managed to enter her bloodstream. My mom flew to India immediately, but her mom never regained consciousness. She never got to say good-bye, and neither did I. I remembered summers with my grandma, when she would share her love of books with me, and tell me stories of surviving the Great Partition between Pakistan and India, and her love for her ten dogs growing up. Panther had died shortly before my grandma, in my arms at the vet's office, when he could no longer eat or walk on his own. They'd both spent years fighting cancer, undergoing relentless treatment and surgery, but it hadn't been enough to save them. My mother's heart seemed permanently broken by the loss; every day she had talked to her mom on the phone before going to sleep. I felt the weight of both my personal loss and my mom's loss as well.

The grief combined with the helplessness uncorked something inside me—that good indignation over the neglected state of women's health—signaling to me that it was finally time to start thinking about my own company and a concept I wanted to work on, even if I needed to continue working full time at my current job to support myself.

Having a mentor like Dave and access to advice from people like Roy Chin were instrumental in helping me take the next steps toward my goals. It also confirmed for me that sometimes the best jobs, at least in the beginning of your career and entrepreneurial journey, are not always the ones that pay the most or offer the most prestige. Sometimes, you have to make short-term sacrifices for long-term gains.

3

While You're Down There

Networking Without a Network

I was lying on my back in nothing but a paper gown, my bare
feet in cold metal stirrups, and staring at the ceiling the first
time I pitched my startup idea. I blurted out, "Hey, so, while
you're down there . . ." I could feel the doctor shift her position
slightly, but I carried on. "I have this catheter concept I'd love to
tell you about!"

I watched Dr. Cooke's head slowly emerge from behind the
white sheet draped across my knees. She had that "deer caught
in the headlights" look in her eyes, visibly taken aback that I was
trying to tell her about a new product while she was in the middle of a pelvic exam. It had been ten years since my own medical
odyssey. I was now twenty-three and hadn't had another ovarian

cyst since college, was working in the medical device field, about to be engaged to Raj, and still obsessed with creating a product to identify cancer. Being in Dr. Cooke's office, my childhood memories came flooding back, but I wanted to move forward. To do that I needed to know that I was developing a product that gynecologists would want to use.

Entrepreneurs sometimes believe that the ultimate validation of their idea comes from an investor who agrees to put money into the concept. In reality, if you're solving a real pain point for your customers, investment will come. Therefore, the most valuable endorsement comes from potential customers. For my particular product, the customer was the gynecologist. Though the patient would ultimately benefit from the device, physicians would be the ones buying and using it. I hadn't yet left the cardiovascular startup I worked for as I didn't quite have the savings to support myself, so I would have to squeeze in these meetings with potential customers before or after my full-time job. The even bigger problem was, I didn't know any gynecologists professionally, as my work experience was in the cardiovascular space. The only gynecologist I knew was my own: the now startled Dr. Cooke.

Before this appointment, I had called her office and asked the receptionist if I could speak to Dr. Cooke about a new catheter concept. The receptionist said no, believing I was yet another vendor trying to sell something. I stressed about it for a week. I was nervous but asked myself: *What was the worst that could happen? If they said no, I would suffer through some (more) rejection. But what was the best-case scenario? I could get the introduction I needed to take the critical next step.* I mustered up the courage and called back. I feigned a stomach ache and asked to see the gynecologist as soon as possible. Appointment granted.

Networking at the start of your career can feel a bit like staring at a blank page. For some of us, just the thought of introducing ourselves to strangers in a large, crowded room or convention hall is the stuff of nightmares. But networking isn't limited to professional happy hours, where you go from person to person shaking hands, business cards at the ready, hoping that something or someone useful will come out of the exercise. Meaningful networking doesn't have to feel like speed dating, nor must it consist of reaching out cold on LinkedIn (though I do recommend trying this if nothing else has worked).

Valuable connections can be made in smaller, more natural situations and through a series of one-on-one conversations with people whom you already know or to whom you have been introduced through colleagues, friends, or even family. You never know where good advice will come from. And if you talk to enough people, you'll get advice that's often conflicting. It's actually beneficial to hear different thoughts and opinions on whatever task is in front of you. But remember: no one knows the situation like you do—so ultimately, go with the advice that resonates most with your gut. Also, sometimes people who are supposed to be "experts" in a certain field tend to be the most jaded about it: they've seen the most failures. I would listen carefully to what they have to say—no need to repeat mistakes—but use your optimism and fresh eyes as a strength. Just because they couldn't figure out a solution doesn't mean that you will not.

Even if your message doesn't land with the first several people you talk to, don't get discouraged—keep reaching out. If you're onto something, someone will find you or your idea compelling, and eventually you'll make a worthwhile connection. The people you meet with don't need to be business superstars. It's a small world, and the people who you talk to may know someone who knows someone relevant—remember the concept of six degrees of separation? That's a legit theory that Microsoft researchers say holds true.

If you're open about what you're working on, you can even take advantage of chance encounters. I once struck up a conversation with the passenger sitting next to me on a plane, and he turned out to be an entrepreneur and offered to look over my presentation during the duration of the flight. A friend of mine grew up in the Midwest and wanted to go into investment banking. The problem was that most banks are located on the coasts, and she didn't know anyone to reach out to. She brought it up in casual conversation with her soccer coach, and it turned out that his cousin worked at an investment bank in New York. He made the connection, and that's how she landed her first job out of school. The key to unlocking the power of serendipity is networking with an open mind. When you're not sure where to start, don't let the feeling of looking at a blank sheet of paper paralyze you. Start anywhere and talk to everyone, and it's simplest to start with someone you know. Just have the conversation.

After spending months upon months reading about ovarian cancer and women's health, I still hadn't found a concept I wanted to pursue related to cancer. But as I did my research, I stumbled upon another unmet need. One of the leading causes of infertility in women is fallopian tube blockages, but the procedure to diagnose it is outdated and inaccurate. I had envisioned a concept I was eager to create—a device that had a camera that would more accurately detect blockages of the fallopian tube. I had only been working for a few years so I needed to surround myself with people who knew about medical devices, maybe even people who had been part of early-stage companies before. Even if I could find people with suitable backgrounds for the tasks ahead, how would I convince them to take a bet on a first-time female founder who was neither an MD nor had years of experience in the medical field? Would they believe that I could execute such a grand plan so early in my career? I pushed the thought of convincing them aside to focus on the task at hand: finding them. I was still working in entry-level positions, which didn't arm me with an impressive Rolodex. Like everyone else in my situation, I had to be creative if I was to build a network from almost nothing.

Dr. Cooke quickly got over her shock at being pitched while examining my pelvic region and kindly offered to discuss my idea outside of the exam room. She agreed to meet in a few days at a café in downtown Saratoga, where I was living at the time, about twenty minutes from her office. Years later, she told me she took time out of her schedule to do so not only because she could see herself using the product but because it was clear to her that my health scare was my driving force. That personal commitment made an impression on her. Sometimes, leaders or entrepreneurs try to dampen their emotions or passion around something because they see it as unprofessional. It's okay to be genuinely excited when talking about something you love, and it often pays off because people feel connected to you.

Before validating your product or solution, you have to

validate the existence of the problem. If you're going to dedicate your life to working on something, make sure that you're working on a problem that needs a solution. That's why, as soon as we sat down at the café, I asked Dr. Cooke what she thought of hysterosalpingography, or HSG, an X-ray test that outlines the shape of the uterus and shows whether the fallopian tubes are blocked. She told me that many of her patients thought the procedure was painful. Other patients would go on to have "miracle babies" after being told that their fallopian tubes were blocked because the HSG had given them the wrong answer. Another drawback to the HSG procedure is that it can't be done in the gynecologist's office as it requires the use of X-ray and dyes, so patients have to make an appointment at a radiology suite. Unless their gynecologist is willing to travel, she or he will be unable to perform the procedure. So, Dr. Cooke hadn't done the procedure in many years.

Dr. Cooke thought I should talk to gynecologists who actively send patients for the procedure and would have recent experiences with it. She introduced me to several other gynecologists, many of whom liked the idea, and several who did not. The ones who didn't like the idea believed that introducing a full catheter with some sort of a camera attached might be too expensive for the health care system to handle, even if it did offer more accurate answers (dye is much less expensive than a small camera). Others simply didn't believe that it would be possible to create a technology that could navigate the fallopian tube without damaging it. If innovators had figured out how to navigate thin blood vessels in the brain, couldn't someone figure out the fallopian tubes? But, alas, other companies had tried creating devices that could visualize the fallopian tubes and had failed. Even when the gynecologist didn't like the concept, I learned from those conversations as much as I did from those with doctors who liked the idea, maybe more. As a result, I was better able to shape exactly what my product would do and how it should do it.

That "negative" feedback proved helpful because it sent me back to find and read patents from previous companies that had tried and failed to develop a way to navigate the fallopian tubes. I also read clinical studies on fallopian tube exploration published by physicians from all over the world. I learned that "camera on a stick" endoscopic catheters faced something called "white-out": There is no light in the fallopian tube, so in addition to having a camera, you need a light source in order to obtain a discernible image. But it wasn't that simple as the light has to be kept a sufficient distance from what you are imaging; otherwise, it would wash out the image. Complicating matters further, the fallopian tube is only 1 millimeter in inner diameter, or about 1/25 of an inch, which doesn't leave a lot of room for lights, camera, or action. Whatever solution I came up with would have to deal with these problems.

Whether or not they liked my idea, the physicians I spoke with respected my intentions enough that they would always offer to introduce me to more doctors. I quickly went from knowing only my gynecologist to knowing dozens of doctors across the country. One of those connections led to Dr. Lynn Westphal, then the head of women's health at Stanford University.

The reproductive unit at Stanford has since moved, but at the time it was located on the basement floor of the hospital.

After waiting for some time for my scheduled meeting, I was led by Dr. Westphal's assistant to her office. Dr. Westphal's reputation as an excellent and sought-after physician preceded her. Her crisp white lab coat and stern but attentive gaze did nothing to assuage my nerves. Yet she turned out to be similar in spirit to my high school teacher Ms. Chetty. While her demeanor was intimidating, she was encouraging, engaged, patient, and committed both to women's health and to helping me. She listened closely to what I wanted to do and then told me that there was a device that allowed for the visualization of the uterus, but not the fallopian tubes, called a hysteroscope. This device has something called a working channel—or an empty passage—that another catheter can be placed into. She suggested that perhaps I could use the working channel of the hysteroscope to access the fallopian tubes, and asked if I wanted to come back in a few days to watch her do the procedure.

After signing the appropriate consent forms, I found myself in Dr. Westphal's outpatient operating room. Before the procedure, the patient was given antianxiety medication. While the section of the hysteroscope that enters the patient isn't that large, *anything* entering a woman's vaginal cavity can be scary. Memories of all the transvaginal ultrasounds I had to undergo as a kid washed over me—I could have used one of those pills myself. Watching the patient go through the procedure reminded me yet again that while the device would be marketed to doctors, my work had to center around the patient.

I also noticed that when a physician does an imaging procedure, they have to look three places at once: first, at their own hands as they guide the device; second, at the patient, to ensure that she is as comfortable as possible; and third, at the screen to check if the images are readable, in order to accurately diagnose what they see. I realized that whatever product I conceptualized would have to be as easy as possible to use to minimize any complications from the procedure itself.

Dr. Westphal agreed to be an informal advisor. This was well before I had a prototype or even a single dollar in funding. In fact, I had only just landed on a name for the company, nVision Medical, because I wanted to envision a future of women's health where our issues were taken seriously. Dr. Westphal shared the same hope. Her position as well as her reputation as a well-respected author of academic papers and speaker at conferences offered credibility and brought more people to the table. Early connections who believe in you and your concept can often lead to the exponential growth of your network, and you never really stop building that network. Within the network that you create, a few people will be the keystones to your success. She was one of my keystones, and when the time was right, her conversations with investors would help me raise the initial seed money I needed to build a prototype.

My series of conversations with physicians also led me to Dr. Viviane Connor, who practices gynecology in Palm Beach, Florida, and specializes in minimally invasive gynecology. "Minimally invasive" means that there is a device that enters the body through natural orifices. You never make a cut with a knife. That's exactly what I was aiming to do at nVision. We wanted to access the length of the fallopian tube by crossing first the vaginal cavity and then the uterus—no incisions. Dr. Connor not only loved the concept of replacing the HSG but years later would bring to my attention a key scientific discovery that helped me figure out our ovarian cancer diagnostic product.

Now that I had spoken with dozens of my target customers and believed that I was onto something, it was time to switch gears and focus on people who could help me build a strong business case for the product. After all, plenty of well-designed products that could serve patients exist but never make it to market because it isn't clear who the real customer is: Who would pay for it and why? And how much are they willing to pay?

When it came to finding the right business advisors, I was really lost—where to start? I was drawing a blank. Luckily, around the same time, one of my closest high school friends, Mallika, asked me to grab a drink. While we shared beers and slurped up noodles at our favorite ramen place, I remembered that her father had started and sold a tech company (this connection was clearly a benefit of living in Silicon Valley; I expect it would usually take a few more meetings to get to someone like Mallika's dad). I asked her if I could ask her dad a few questions over a family dinner. The Bhandarkars's place always felt cozy and welcoming, and it was somewhere I had gone so often it felt like a second home. As we sat at their dining table, complete with casual bench seating, and over a drool-inducing home-cooked Indian veggie meal, her dad relayed his entrepreneurial experiences.

After arriving in the US with a degree in computer science, he built a business software that thousands of people use around the world. While his story inspired me and he wanted to be helpful, unfortunately, he wasn't in my field and couldn't think of any useful introductions. Mallika's mom had a personal interest in helping up-and-coming Indian women and offered to introduce me to a family friend who was working on clinical trials for drugs in India. But we were years away from clinical trials, and working on a device instead of a drug, with no intention of doing any testing in India, so it wasn't an entirely natural fit. I wasn't in a position to be choosy, so I took it as an opportunity to talk to someone in health care at least. After several fruitful meetings where the contact and I discussed everything from the name of the company to potential first investors, she offered to introduce me to Anula Jayasuriya, at the time a partner at Evolvence, a venture capital firm that primarily invests in India-based startups.

Anula and I planned to meet one day in late December 2009, in Los Altos (a city that many of the Silicon Valley's most successful call home) at the Starbucks on Main Street, without much correspondence beforehand. She was outside when I arrived, and as I approached her to say hello, she said she was waiting for someone else, turning away. I knew what she looked like, as I always spend time reading about someone online before meeting them in person. This kind of prep work is one way of letting people know that I take them and their time seriously and that we will have a focused discussion. Anula had the right background to be helpful, and I wasn't going to allow her initial snub to deter me. I took a few steps toward her and awkwardly introduced myself. By her startled expression, I think she was expecting someone older, but she quickly recovered and we sat down.

Anula is an MD PhD and holds an MBA, all from Harvard University. When I met her, she was in her early fifties, dressed in fashionable leather pants, her eyes outlined in thick, blue liner, a stark contrast to my gray slacks and makeup-free face. Later I would realize this was a rather tame look for her because she'd often show up to formal events wearing brightly patterned clothing by designers showcased at Neiman Marcus, her favorite store. Anula was known for having filet mignon every night for dinner, which she would wash down with white wine diluted with sparkling water.

Despite my boring attire and awkward introduction, Anula and I hit it off. She believed that women's health was a profoundly underserved area and thought that I might be able to do something about it. Because of her fund's focus on India, it couldn't invest in my idea. However, she offered to help me sharpen my story and translate it to a slide deck, which I would ultimately use to pitch the most important concepts behind the company to investors. Once she thought the deck was good enough—which was no short order; we worked on it for months to reach her standard—she introduced me to relevant investors. In fact, she connected me to every single person who invested in my first round of funding.

Anula was one of the first professional women to whom I grew close. The cardiovascular device startup I worked for was mostly staffed with men, and though I had women as my direct bosses at Abbott, I had never really found a role model. Anula called herself my "360-degree" advisor and wanted to help with more than just my company. A good advisor doesn't just provide strictly professional, operational advice. They know that you are a person trying to have a full life and can help answer questions like *How am I supposed to have a baby and run this company at the same time?* It was Anula whom I called (after 911) when my parents got into a car accident, their car sitting at the bottom of a ditch just off the road (Dad wasn't injured; Mom had a badly broken nose). Anula became my sounding board, and sometimes we disagreed violently. She's more academic than I am and prefers open and unstructured discussions when it comes to big company decisions. I, on the other hand, like to have a specific plan to discuss. Whatever our differences, I knew Anula would be there when things got rough, and they often did.

Anula didn't have enough ego to believe that only her advice would be sufficient to create a successful company, so she helped expand my advisor network. She introduced me to Karen Drexler, who had been an executive at LifeScan, which was acquired by Johnson & Johnson. She was also the former president and CEO of Amira Medical, a glucose-monitoring company that was sold to Roche in 2001. She had great corporate and leadership experience and was also passionate about women's health. While Anula had experience on the investor side, Karen was an operator—someone on the ground, building the company. She had scaled a team and sold a company before. Balancing the backgrounds of the people you bring on as advisors is important.

I was lucky in that many of the potential advisors I met with wanted to learn more about the opportunity my device represented. I'm often asked what I did to attract them to the table. It started with taking their time seriously. For example, as I mentioned with Anula, I always researched someone before meeting them. Because information is so easily available on the internet, you're almost expected to research someone online before meeting them. I found out what type of things they were most interested in professionally and how their particular experiences were a good fit for what I was trying to do. This created a more informed and efficient discussion when we met. People are more inclined to roll up their sleeves and spend time with you if they know that time won't be wasted and will amount to something they care about. Help paint that picture for them. Think about how frustrating it would be if someone asks you for a meeting, then stares at you blankly, without knowing why exactly they asked to meet with you, besides the fact that you are successful and therefore must be able to help them in some way that they can't describe.

Next, I would follow up with every person who had taken the time to talk to me. Not just with a bland thank-you note, but to address any questions or concerns I either couldn't answer or wanted to expand on after the meeting. I wrote a follow-up email to Anula the same day I met her, linking several websites to support certain claims I made during the meeting. I then forwarded the same email to Rajeev, saying, "What do you think of this email? It took me forty-five minutes to write, ha-ha." Turned out to be worth every minute. Not only because she appreciated the answers I provided to her questions and as a result, agreed to meet with me again, but also because when you take the time to answer others' questions thoroughly, you often learn yourself.

A strategic question Anula asked me early on was who in the medical device industry still had a women's-health arm, as many of them had shut down their women's health divisions after a series of failures. Nine years before the acquisition, I pointed out that Boston Scientific had an interest in women's health, as did companies like Johnson & Johnson, Cook Medical, and Karl Storz. This question compelled me to dig deeper into what specifically led so many large companies to shutter these businesses, and I discovered it was because of significant litigation that often cost more than $1 billion. Gynecologists often get sued because of the high-risk work they do with pregnant women. More reason to keep the device and procedure simple to use — but not a reason to stop!

As I continued to meet with potential customers and business advisors, Anula and Karen pointed out that before I could fundraise, I needed to put engineering resources in place that would help me build the product I had in mind. They said that it would be best if the engineers were credible and experienced, people whom investors would trust. Some of the talented engineers I worked with at Abbott immediately jumped to mind.

To my surprise, none of the female engineers whom I had worked with were interested. It might have been because they did not want to leave what they had fought so hard to achieve. They had to endure all-male engineering classes with maybe just a handful of other women, and then compete fiercely for a job at a Fortune 500 company. Of course, they may not have been interested because they simply felt more secure and comfortable at a larger, more established company and didn't want to work for an inexperienced founder.

With that, I started talking to the men I had worked with next. This set off one rejection after another. They would talk to me for a while and then tell me that they weren't interested but without being able to articulate why. Finally, an engineer who had left Abbott to join another startup expressed some interest. Let's call him Michael. We met several times and even filed a patent together that covered a standard endoscope for the fallopian tubes, but that had different umbrellalike features at the end of it to prevent the light source from getting too close to the tissue we wanted to image. Then suddenly, he simply stopped responding to my emails or calls.

I had to continue to brainstorm on my own. If a rigid endoscope was too harsh for the fallopian tube, then what would the fallopian tube be able to tolerate? I was reading the news one day when I saw an article about a "pill camera" used to diagnose digestive issues. During this procedure, called capsule endoscopy, a patient swallows a pill that contains a camera. As the pill travels through the esophagus and digestive tract, it takes images. Though it's a truly shitty situation, you can retrieve the pill and assess the images.

I thought to myself, *A pill shape is smooth—it shouldn't damage the fallopian tube. But how would it travel through it? Well, what if we used water pressure to move it forward, and had it attached to a fishing-line type of mechanism to retrieve it once it got to the end? We could put the camera and the light source in the center of the pill to prevent the issue of white-out.* Because we would be using hydraulic pressure, perhaps it would be simple to use as well. It sounded like science fiction, but I was excited to give it a try and file another patent around the idea.

I emailed Michael again because I wanted to use some of his engineering drawings that we had used in our previous patent to illustrate the difference in what I was doing. Because of this, I wanted to put his name on the patent, though I now know that using previous drawings wouldn't qualify him as an author. I reached out relentlessly, email after email, feeling dejected and believing that he deemed the effort unworthy. Ironically, I didn't hear back until many years later, after my company was acquired, when he called me, asking me why his name wasn't on the patent. He was supposedly shocked when I told him how many times I had emailed him and never heard back. While I was once unimportant enough to ignore, when I was successful, I was on speed dial.

The good news is I had what felt like a brilliant idea and a new way to navigate the fallopian tube without damaging it. Now I needed to focus on how to move forward and start fundraising as quickly as possible—except that I still didn't have an engineer on the team and needed to spend time understanding the size of my market better. I reached out to my network, and Mallika's mom introduced me to a former colleague who then introduced me to Serge Bierhuizen. With a degree in optical engineering, Serge had been working in that field for almost two decades. He was interested in the project, so we started brainstorming on how to create a camera in a pill form.

Now that Serge was helping with the camera element, I still needed help with the catheter portion of the device. After exhausting my network, I decided to get a quote from an outsource design-manufacturing company called Accel. While I could ideate around the catheter and come up with the concept, I knew there were better people out there to actually assemble the product. Also, investors wanted to know how much it would cost to build the catheter I had in mind, so I would present Accel's proposal to those interested. Again, when networking doesn't go your way, you've got to keep your options open and be creative. Meet and talk to everyone you can. Yes, there will be dead ends, but there will also be unexpected pathways. I have known entrepreneurs with few social or professional connections who reached out to anyone who "might know someone who might know someone." And even when they knew no one at all, they used LinkedIn and did a cold outreach with a simple introduction to what they were doing. Eventually, they discovered the right person, and that person helped lead to the next person, and so on.

I also always advise leaders to bring their technical talent in-house, but if you can't have your first choice, go for your second—anything is better than standing still. (Caveat: If you're hiring a full-time employee, you want to take your time to find the right person, and we'll get into that more soon.) In this case, I hired an outside firm to handle this part of the project so I didn't delay being able to start doing research on the concept. With clinician and business advisors now in my corner, and an outsourced manufacturing firm that could help me build the product, I now needed someone who could get into the nitty-gritty and help me create extensive Excel models to demonstrate just how large the market opportunity was, and how we were going to get the product to that market.

Anula knew someone who had his own consulting practice and had worked on these types of commercialization plans for almost thirty years; let's call him John. I met with him and liked him but didn't yet have money to pay him. He saw potential in what we were doing, so he agreed not to charge me for consulting, which consisted of meeting occasionally to provide advice and help create the models we needed.

Through reading papers and talking to physicians, John and I concluded that almost a million HSG procedures (the test we were trying to rep_ace) are done in the United States annually. HSG procedures cost anywhere from $250 to $1,000 each. Only some insurance companies in some states would pay for the procedure, leaving many patients to pay out of pocket. That meant we wanted to price our alternative procedure at a reasonable level, while also considering that since the device was going to be a lot more expensive to make than dye, we needed to cover our costs. We landed on a price point of $750. In terms of how best to get to market, we realized that only a subset of gynecologists already had hysteroscopic equipment (remember: we were going to utilize the channel in the hysteroscope to reach the fallopian tubes) in their offices and that we would need to start by targeting those who did.

One evening, John and I met for dinner in Palo Alto to discuss the latest work he put together around the size of the international market. I appreciated that he would give up his evening—it was hard for me to meet during the day, since I was still working at the cardiovascular device company full time. It was challenging to juggle the demands of both, but I made it work by drawing clear boundaries. If I was at work, I focused on that, and then worked on nVision after hours, staying up until 2:00 or 3:00 in the morning if I had to. After we finished talking through the models and he put his laptop away, we caught up on our personal lives, and he enthusiastically talked about his family and kids. As we stood to leave the restaurant, he leaned over and gave me a sudden kiss on the cheek.

This came as a surprise because up until that moment, John had always been appropriate with me during the several months we knew each other. He was three decades my senior, so I wanted to believe that this spontaneous show of affection was the benign emotion of a man older than my father. I called Anula and relayed the incident to her. She said that even if it were a kind gesture rather than a sexual advance, it was inappropriate. A decade before the #MeToo movement, these sorts of situations weren't discussed openly, and women had long tolerated this kind of behavior. I felt a bit crazy—maybe I was just reading into it too much? But the encounter made me feel off. Uneasy.

It wasn't the first time this kind of thing had happened. I remembered my full-time employer generously inviting me to attend the biggest medical device conference in cardiovascular health, Transcatheter Cardiovascular Therapeutics Conference (TCT). After this conference, like with most conferences, people grabbed drinks at a nearby bar to network and catch up. A group of us ended up at the W Hotel bar, and I felt grateful because it gave me a chance to spend some time with the leaders of the company. At the crowded bar, after one executive struggled to get the attention of the bartender, he turned to me and said, "Surbhi, show some leg." Up until that moment, though I was surrounded by men, I felt like any other coworker. I felt respected and seen as an equal. After the comment, I became confused and overwhelmed. *Was the executive actively thinking about how I was a woman, how I was different?* When something like this happens, you might wonder: Should you brush it off as a joke? Are you overdramatizing? It clearly impacted me, and I can still see the moment, frozen in time, like someone took a photo, like it happened yesterday. Leaders have to be aware of power dynamics and create environments where a diverse set of people feel safe and respected.

John was helping me pro bono and knew the Excel models he put together better than anyone. I had been to his house, met his dogs, and heard about his kids. I decided to give him the benefit of the doubt and continued to meet with him, but only during the day in public locations.

At this point, only a small number of entrepreneurs in women's health medical devices had had any success, and I thought it might be good to connect with a couple of them. John had worked with one of them, let's call him Sean, in the past. John set up a meeting with the three of us at his house in Palo Alto. I knew that Sean continued to innovate in women's health, so beforehand, I asked him to sign a mutual nondisclosure agreement (NDA) to protect the details of the innovation. A mutual NDA is supposed to ensure that neither party shares nor uses any confidential information that is discussed. He didn't respond, but on the day of the meeting, Sean immediately assured me that he had simply forgotten to sign the NDA and that he would get it to me as soon as he arrived home. Not only did I believe him, but I was overjoyed and surprised that he was willing to spend time with me.

With John's dogs enthusiastically barking in the backyard, we began our meeting. I described my product, and Sean's body language and demeanor—leaning forward, mindfully engaged—indicated that he was excited. He gave me great advice about how to advance the product, including that once I had a prototype, I could study it on human uteruses that had been removed from the patient for medical reasons. That would offer a better sense as to how the catheter would react once it was inside a person. He shared some of the challenges that he had faced when starting a women's health company, such as the lack of investor interest and the limited number of companies still actively investing in women's health. As we closed the meeting, he asked me to reach out to him anytime for advice or even another meeting, and again emphasized that he would return the NDA to me later that day.

I emailed him three times after that, and he never responded, never returned the NDA. Years later, even when we ran into each other at conferences, he would turn and hurry off in the other direction. I wonder if he didn't want others crowding his field, though I never saw having other upstarts as competition. The more innovators in the field of women's health, the better.

After being repeatedly ditched by men, it dawned on me that most of my early supporters were women. Perhaps they better related to the problem I was trying to solve, or perhaps they could relate to me better. Most of them had achieved amazing feats in their careers, but few if any had been bestowed with the brand name that many of their male counterparts had despite their similar accomplishments. The women who supported me early on in my journey continue to support me even today. Today's social media–fueled society makes us believe that one of the most desirable achievements is to be seen with bright and shiny people; we are often judged by the company we keep. In the startup ecosystem or any professional world, certain people are viewed as rock stars of that industry. So when starting a career, some often think that those people hold the keys to the kingdom and can magically elevate them to success. Those are the people they try to aim for when networking. And of course, these particular people might be helpful—but it is more likely that they are impossible to reach or too busy to join you, even if you can get in touch with them. As long as someone has the right expertise to help, you shouldn't care how Insta-famous they are or how well recognized their name is.

Admittedly, brand names can be hard to resist. They are seductive. For me, that brand name was Harvard. Anula drew my attention to the Harvard New Venture Competition, to which hundreds of entrepreneurs submit business plans. A committee then selects three plans that they believe have the greatest potential to become promising companies. After that, they ask the three entrepreneurs to pitch in front of a panel of judges, who select one winner. I thought it might be a great opportunity to expand my network.

I started writing the business plan. After more than a year of research, it flowed out of me easily. I didn't even need to look at an example. I wanted the business plan to describe what made me believe that replacing the HSG with a more accurate method to diagnose fallopian tube blockage was a good idea, why I was dedicating all of my time to solving this problem. I put pen to paper, and then Anula and I edited it together for hours while sitting around her kitchen table. A few weeks after submitting the proposal, I got the call that I had made it to the top three. After a series of defeats with advisors and engineers, it felt good.

There was one catch. I honest to goodness missed that you have to be an alum in order to apply. Anula had received multiple degrees from Harvard, and when I filled out the application, I put her name on it as an advisor. The reviewers missed that she wasn't a cofounder working at nVision or working on it full time.

After telling me that I would be pitching in front of an audience of several hundred people and a panel of six venture capitalists, they realized I hadn't attended Harvard Business School (HBS) or Harvard. But it was too late, they had already turned down all of the other proposals. So they broke their own rules this one time, and let me go forward.

Leading up to the competition, I was incredibly nervous not only about the content of my presentation but also about what I was going to wear. I knew that while I was taking the brain-power to think about this, men were using that time to prepare. Knowing that I wasn't a graduate from the right school to begin with put more pressure on me—what would I wear to make them take me seriously? I called my much more fashionable younger sister, Swasti, and she happily agreed to help me find an outfit. My mom, Swasti, and I went to the local mall and ended up at Ann Taylor. Swasti selected suitable black dress pants. Next, she helped me choose a blouse with a light blue floral pattern that wasn't too feminine because I didn't want to scare the men and not too masculine so I didn't scare the men. A beige blazer with rolled sleeves completed the look. This effort represented the most time I'd ever given to thinking about an outfit.

On the day of the competition, my anxiety skyrocketed. It was my first time presenting in front of a few hundred people. As I climbed on the stage of the Hiller Aviation Museum in San Carlos, I only heard buzzing in my ears. Afterward, though I re-member little about it, Raj told me that the talk was electrify-ing; my nervousness came across as intensity and passion in a good way. The blazer turned out to be a fortuitous choice be-cause I sweated through my shirt. When the pitch competition ended, the venture capitalist judges disappeared into a private room to deliberate. After fifteen minutes or so, they reemerged, announcing a tie for top place: three votes for my pitch and three for another pitch centered around mining precious metals out of trash. The founder was another Indian American woman with a background more impressive than mine and who actually did go to Harvard Business School. The judges decided to open the standoff to audience voting. Despite all of my competitor's friends in the audience, I lost the "popular" vote by only one person.

A few days later, I called the woman who organized the pitch competition to thank her for the experience. She was still upset that I hadn't gone to HBS. She told me that I simply was not polished enough and that I would never be as polished as an HBS grad, or as successful, so I should apply as soon as possible. This critique fed into my deepest insecurities. Perhaps I didn't have the pedigree needed to chase the lofty goal I had set for myself. Maybe I didn't have the gravitas. To make matters worse, there was a fallout from my loss at the competition: two male engineers I had been pursuing to join nVision had attended the competition and promptly left the project after my public defeat. Although I never discussed it with them, perhaps they felt I wasn't leadership material if I couldn't pull off a win at the Harvard face-off.

Frankly, I was embarrassed. It was my first time speaking publicly, and it felt like I had failed in front of a huge audience. I didn't know how to respond when audience members came up to me and said, "I thought for sure you were going to win, what you're working on is so important." Maybe I wasn't good enough to carry such an important product forward. And it wasn't just the audience I was worried about; all of my friends and family knew that I was part of this competition.

I had to sit with the feelings of loss and rejection for a day or two before that good indignation washed over me. I mean, what was I doing all of this for, anyway? Was it to "win" every step of the way? Be announced as the Harvard Business School entrepreneur of the year? No. It was to help patients, even if I had to do it one baby step at a time. I shut out the voices of the naysayers at the competition and instead focused on all of the conversations with physicians and patients telling me how badly they needed this product. I stopped focusing on the fact that I ultimately lost the competition and instead realized that, despite being underqualified, I had made it to the final three. The discomfort wasn't an unfamiliar feeling for me. Even when the other kids made me feel embarrassed about playing with bugs, I didn't stop. Was I going to quit now? No. If someone chooses to be an entrepreneur, the failure is often broadcasted. I finally realized that the only person thinking about my life and my career every minute of the day was me. I had to be happy with what I was doing. The haters were going to spend maybe a few minutes thinking about it or chuckling about it. Why would I allow that to inform my decision about what to tackle with my entire being? That's the advantage of working on something not for the sake of a potential payout or for the sake of a title, but because you feel strongly about the problem you are solving. Even in that hard moment, I knew that I wanted to continue to dedicate my life to working on women's health. Plus, the competition let me see who really cared about the concept as much as I did, and who believed in me.

Corinne Nevinny, another of my business advisors whom Anula had introduced me to, flew up from Los Angeles for a few hours to support me during the pitch competition. I had met Corinne, a pioneer in the medical device industry, in December 2009, at what turned out to be an auspicious lunch that would help with my fundraising. Her reputation preceded her. In 2006, when the health care field was even more male-dominated than it is today, Corinne had served on the board of Edwards Lifesciences, then became their chief financial officer and treasurer, and then took an operational role as president of global operations in charge of all manufacturing around the world as well as all functional areas. After leaving Edwards, she sat on a variety of science and pharmaceutical company boards and had begun a small venture fund to support women entrepreneurs called LMN VC.

Before the competition, I picked her up from the airport and was intimidated as she walked toward me—how successful she was, how she carried herself with so much grace and confidence (she'd gone to HBS, after all). She immediately asked me to recite my pitch and we practiced together on the way to the competition. At that point in my career, I hadn't done a lot of public speaking, so it was a big deal to rehearse and drive at the same time. Though she saw me lose, it didn't sway her dedication to me—in fact, I think it may have made her double down on her commitment. She also believed that patients needed my device, so if others weren't going to help out, she was going to be the one to step up to the plate. Her involvement was critical to our upcoming fundraising efforts.

Although she was unquestionably accomplished, she was less known than her male counterparts. In a way, she, too, was underrated. As you go through your journey as someone who feels the weight of doubt, be careful not to underrate others who have been overlooked by naysayers. Instead, cultivate a network of people who believe in you, regardless of how other people might feel about them. Be thorough and respect people's time when you meet or are introduced to a potential contact. Trajectory-altering relationships and connections may come from it.

It might sound like I ran into quite a few bad seeds during my initial networking to get my company off the ground, and it's true—I had to kiss some frogs (and one of them kissed me). The underrated can expect to be overlooked more often than not. But the thing with startups and career success more broadly is that you don't need everyone to believe in you. You just need a few people with the right backgrounds and enough conviction to allow you to stand on their shoulders. If you keep those people close by providing them an inside look not only on your wins but your losses, they will be invested and continue to stay by your side.

Despite the rejections, I now had a group of credible clinical advisors who confirmed that they would use the product once it existed; an experienced optical engineer and an outsourced engineering firm that would help me with the product; and well-respected, committed business advisors to help me revise my business model and make introductions to investors. Now all I needed was someone to write me a check. How hard could that be?

4

Fundraising

Telling a Story and
Developing a Thick Skin

September 9, 2011, was an especially warm Boston day, and it took this California girl who thought the East Coast was always cold by surprise. I was overdressed in heavy black slacks and blazer, and a crisp, plain-collared shirt, all under a woolen winter coat in a lame attempt to look older and more sophisticated. I walked down the bustling riverside Atlantic Avenue with Darshana Zaveri, a venture capitalist from Catalyst Health. I had been trying to convince her to invest in nVision for more than a year.

Darshana's firm focused on early-stage funding of disruptive solutions for unmet health care needs, which made her a perfect potential investor for my business. I had been trying to meet her in person for a year and a half, so that we were finally together in Boston was a big deal.

A year earlier, in January of 2010, Anula had introduced me to Darshana when I set out to raise my first round of funding, $250,000. Though it would be the smallest amount of capital I would raise in a fundraising round, it was the most challenging because it was so early in the process of building the business. My initial phone call with Darshana captured her interest but not enough to do a deal. Over the next several months, I provided her with an endless amount of information—future potential financial statements, the size of the market, operating plans, budgets, introductions to physicians—anything I thought would be helpful. After digging into the opportunity extensively, Darshana finally invited me to meet her and her partners at a law office in Boston. She told me that despite being in the beginning stages of the company and not yet having much to show, she was impressed by my thoroughness.

The meeting was held in an imposing building on the Charles River—which was originally named Quinobequin by the native Massachusetts tribe, meaning "meandering" as the river doubles back on itself several times along its eighty-mile length. I hoped this wouldn't become a metaphor for my fundraising journey. We entered the building and rode the elevator to the grand reception area where I was about to pitch to her partnership. Darshana led the way into the room while I tried to control my breathing.

The past year and a half had been rough, and this was one of my last opportunities to raise money. I had completely exhausted not only all my own connections but Anula's as well. At least fifty investors had turned me down, and while I took the elevator up to the tenth floor, I struggled to block out all those rejections. One involved a prominent venture capitalist in Palo Alto, whom I recalled leaning so far back in his chair that I was afraid he would fall over. As I introduced myself, he plucked a plastic-wrapped candy from a bowl sitting on the conference room table. Every time I spoke, he played with the wrapper intentionally, the crinkling sound deafening in the small room. It unnerved me. If his actions were a test, I did not pass. I blanked on his simple questions, and Anula had to dive in to try to save me. (I now know that fundraising with an advisor present isn't a good idea as you should demonstrate to a potential investor that you're confident enough to try and stand on your own two feet.)

I shook my head, trying to get rid of the memory, but a mix-tape of rejections played as we approached our floor: *Women's health is a niche market. You don't yet have a prototype. You're not a doctor or a formally trained engineer. You don't have a graduate degree.* The list went on. I steadied my mind and managed to drown out my anxieties by calling on that old indignation and the conversations I had had with gynecologists about how much this product was needed. I knew how necessary innovation was from those conversations, research, and my own experience. Recalling how far I'd come since high school, I was flooded with memories of times I was told that I would never achieve a goal or dream, but I followed my own path. It bolstered me. By the time we arrived at the doors of the conference room, I had managed to quiet the noise. I left my psychological baggage at the door and focused on the meeting in front of me. I've found that learning how to calm my mind with simple techniques—like controlling my breath and acknowledging my doubts, while also knowing what positive thoughts I can call upon to block out the negative—can help in high-pressure situations.

As Darshana opened the conference room doors, there was a familiar sight: a large white room appointed with carefully chosen corporate art. A perfectly fitting rectangular table the size of a small Caribbean island stood in the middle, accessorized by three white men leaning back in their chairs. They looked up at me and smiled in a friendly way, and I wondered what type of first impression I made, weighed down as I was by multiple layers of clothing. Even if the particular people in front of you are prejudice-free, the problem with unconscious bias is that you will expend some mental energy sorting through whether biases exist in whatever current situation you are in. While it's fine to acknowledge that it might be a possibility, you should try to recognize as quickly as possible that there's also a chance it may not exist. You can't let negative assumptions or realities affect your ability to do your best. Focus on the task at hand. Don't worry about what other people might be thinking, because you really do not know. Assuming everyone is against you is a recipe for failure.

I know this is controversial advice. Am I really saying to acknowledge that someone might be sexist or biased in some other way, but then just to let it slide? Who am I to comment on this particular problem anyway, when other demographic groups have it so much worse? Look, I don't have all the answers, and this is something I struggle with talking about every time I'm asked about it. But ultimately, building a business is hard enough. I hate to place the burden of changing the world on the shoulders of women and minorities also trying to build their own ladders. There are small things you can do along the way. For example, never feel pressure to laugh at a joke you find offensive. If you see a male colleague interrupting a female one repeatedly, go ahead and gently cut him off: "Bob, I think Sally was trying to say something." But calling someone out in the moment will rarely get you what you want and will cause you to lose track of your immediate objective. As Beyoncé says, "The best revenge is your paper." Kidding aside, if you're able to focus and win, you will be another example of a woman killing it out there, which is something this world needs more of.

Trying to focus on the moment and opportunity in front of me, I fumbled through my backpack, pulled out my laptop, and went through the awkward ritual that entrepreneurs go through before every pitch—attempting to connect to a projector or TV you've never seen before while everyone stares at you. Once I was set up, I proceeded to take the investors through my presentation, beginning with my motivation for starting the company, the cancer scare that happened so long ago, then talking about the clinical need and how much we could help patients with this product, how many patients in the US alone there are (market size), our regulatory and reimbursement pathway, competitive landscape, and other relevant details. At that point, I had practiced the pitch so many times that I was on autopilot when delivering it. This gave me an opportunity to pay attention to my audience's body language and adjust my pitch in response as needed. During this meeting, I could see Darshana's team intently lean forward when I talked about the clinical need for the device, so I made sure to go over that section more deeply. They were fully engaged, which made me even more enthusiastic. I was taking them on a journey, and their facial expressions hinted that they were connecting to my message. I could see that my indignation over the dismal reality of women's health was starting to become their indignation.

When I first began to fundraise for nVision, I didn't have much beyond a well-thought-out plan, a couple of engineering resources, deep subject matter expertise on the disease I wanted to address, and a thick skin. My passion for what I was doing and my good indignation, coupled with these building blocks, would have to be enough to create a compelling story, a narrative convincing enough that others would pay attention and then stay engaged.

When pitching or describing a topic, it's easy to rattle off facts about the marketplace opportunity or the exact approach you'll take when creating your patent portfolio. But remember that investors, potential advisors, and employees are all people, and people are easily bored. Instead of simply bullet-pointing your ideas, engage your audience with a story that helps them understand what you're trying to achieve relevant to their interests. It is possible to find interesting transitions between even the most seemingly mundane facts, weaving them into a compelling narrative. Why are *you* excited about the opportunity? Can you figure out a way to make them feel this excitement? Before there was you and your company, there was a history related to the problem you are solving. Then you came in, and you're trying to do something new and different. And then there are the next couple of years ahead of you. How are you going to make it all come together? The people considering your idea are giving you their most valuable asset—their time—so make it count. When you pitch, describe the problem in such a way that people can feel that the issue you are solving is real. Remember: you're making the case that they should choose your company or project over other opportunities.

After the meeting ended, we said our good-byes, and Darshana walked me back to my rental car. She seemed as happy as I was. She told me that she, too, felt like the meeting couldn't have gone better and thought that she was likely to call me the following day with good news. This time, there was no controlling the pounding of my heart. I was elated but trying to remain measured, not wanting to get ahead of myself even though it was hard not to.

When I got into my car, I sat for a minute to let my nerves cool and enjoy the warm sunshine on my face. Finally, I turned the engine on and drove to my hotel in Cambridge, which was on the other end of the river. I was so frugal back then that I always used Priceline to bid on hotel rooms, which had you pick a geographic area, and then its software would match you with a hotel room in that general vicinity. Once back at the hotel, I quickly grabbed my bags and raced to the airport. I finally settled into my airplane seat and promptly passed out.

Arriving home at 1:00 a.m. after a long and exhausting day, I couldn't fall asleep. I went back over every detail of the pitch in my head, turning on my bedside lamp to jot down notes on questions I maybe could have answered better. Eventually, the sun trickled into the bedroom, which was my cue to start staring at my phone, willing Darshana to call. If this didn't work out, I didn't know anyone else I could approach for fundraising.

Eventually, the phone rang. "Surbhi, I am sorry to say I couldn't push my team over the finish line. They are all excited about the concept and you, but in terms of a spectrum of risk, well, you're a first-time entrepreneur, without a prototype, without, well, too much of anything . . . we just can't make the investment." I drew the curtains and climbed back into bed. I let all the feelings of rejection and doubt run through my veins, under my skin, into my heart. *It's over*, I thought to myself.

Being strong doesn't mean that you don't feel emotion. Sometimes, your emotions are so strong that they wash over you, and you have no choice but to accept them. Other times, we go into a mode of self-protection and tell ourselves it's better to feel nothing than to feel disappointed, rejected, or downcast. But in these cases, the easy path isn't always the right one, and things might need to feel a bit harder before they get easier. The more an emotion is in the periphery, nagging at you, the longer you will spend on it and the less efficient you'll be at achieving the task at hand.

After accepting and feeling all my negative emotions, my mind finally began to clear. I could reflect on the phone conversation a bit more rationally. Darshana had said no, but it was with much reluctance. I knew she wished she was calling with good news. I slowly sat up in bed, grabbed the pen and paper on my nightstand, and started to formulate a plan.

Seeking something elusive like funding for a startup or a high-level leadership position in any industry will generally have a similar pattern: tell a good story, get rejected, tell a good story, get rejected. And on it goes until your story finally resonates with someone. The fact is that fundraising tends to be a difficult experience for most entrepreneurs. Even if the money comes quickly, it might have come with a blow to the ego, a hard negotiation, or a caveat. What makes the entire experience even more surprising is the story the media often tells of quick, easy fundraising, which despite how it's portrayed, is rare. This misperception can make newcomers think that the winners in life get checks written easily, so their own difficulties scraping together money must be their own fault. Self-doubt and the skepticism of others can make this already difficult process even more draining because it feels even harder to break through.

If you feel underrated, you need to be better than those who are privileged—more knowledgeable. quicker thinking, and stronger. It's the unfair reality. Sometimes, you can fight against the system from the outside. Other times, you have to play by certain rules to break into the existing system in order to get what you need—and then, eventually, work on changing the system. As unfortunate as the situation is, you have to be more prepared than others to achieve the same level of attention and respect. You won't always be given the benefit of the doubt like others might.

After spending a few hours with pen and pad in hand, I called Darshana back and told her that I would take a big risk, too, if she took a risk on me. I was so confident in the idea and so invested in making it work that I said I wouldn't draw a salary for two years, that I would either move back home or rely on Rajeev if I had to (a privileged position to be in, to be sure). I explained why I wanted her specifically as a partner—she was thorough, understood the clinical need, and she and I got along. After hearing this, Darshana knew that I was willing to make the company work no matter what the obstacle might be, that I was all in and didn't need a contingency plan. That was enough for Darshana; she hung up the phone and started working on her team, trying to walk them through the merits of the deal. Again, they said no. Then, she got a bit more aggressive—she asked them to either invest in my company or make an exception to her contract with them so she could invest in me on her own.

I try to picture what that meeting must have been like for Darshana, being the only woman in the firm, not yet a partner. She was just establishing herself as a venture capitalist. She is also brown, standing up to established men who were also a full head taller than her. Something about the nVision concept, my passion for it, and our personal connection compelled her to go back to the table. Eventually, she made the phone call that she wanted to make the first time: she finally had a yes from her partnership to invest in nVision. I had successfully empowered my underrated champion, and she had stuck out her neck for me. That's how I raised my first $100,000 and found a lifetime business ally and friend.

Perhaps because business was a man's game for such a long time, empathy and emotions are highly underrated in the professional world. If I hadn't felt the disappointment and pain of Darshana's rejection and used those emotions to reenergize my commitment to the project, I may not have kept at it. If I had run away from those complex emotions or let them defeat me, I might have lost steam. If I didn't let myself feel the excitement of the product's genuine potential to change a sector of women's health care, I would not have had the persistence required to execute the plan. And if I didn't have empathy, it would have been impossible for me to empower Darshana to realize the legitimacy of her view of the company—and to try again.

Rejection is part of the process of success. Not everyone will respond to your ideas the way you do. It doesn't matter. What matters is how *you* react to it. I believe that the old, stoic style of leadership, where emotional expression was not encouraged, is on its way out the door. Acknowledging our emotions to ourselves and others makes us better leaders.

My nearly missed opportunity came with a caveat. Darshana wanted to invest, but I also had to find at least one other interested investor before her firm would give me a dime. While I was initially stumped, I recalled the meeting I had had with Corinne Nevinny, the medical device pioneer. I contacted her again now, and she agreed to have lunch with me on an especially rainy day in Burlingame. I pushed through the Asian fusion restaurant's front doors as quickly as I could, thoroughly drenched and embarrassingly fifteen minutes late. She had one of her partners with her, an HBS classmate named Linda Greub, an accomplished business development professional in health care.

When I made it to their table, after leaving a trail of micro puddles behind me, the two of them were positioned so that when I sat down, they were directly across from me. I felt my anxiety flare up and I beat myself up for my tardiness. Corinne's presidential demeanor exacerbated my insecurities further. Linda was sharp, firing question after question at me as I talked through the story and promise of nVision. They later turned to each other to have a candid conversation in front of me: "Corinne, who is going to fund this women's health idea, especially with a female, first-time entrepreneur at the helm?" asked Linda. "Well, I guess if we think it's a good idea, we'll have to be the ones who support it, right?" responded Corinne. These two women had given me a gift of their confidence and time, and I felt invigorated.

I put Darshana and Corinne together, and their respective firms both decided to take the plunge. Finally, after one year and eleven months of fundraising, three women were willing to put in a total of $250,000, which also included a small check from Anula. The $250,000 would be given to me in two parts, or tranches: $125,000 to start, and once I had a working prototype, they would give me another $125,000. Anula, Darshana, Corinne, and I made up our all-female board.

The untold story of nVision is a story of women supporting women. When I first came up with the concept for nVision in 2009 and wrote my first patent, and three years later when I started the company in 2012, corporate feminism wasn't talked about much in mainstream media. The word *femtech* had not yet been coined, and male investors would sometimes refer to women's health as "bikini medicine." It's still hard to run a women's health company, no matter what you call it.

In December of 2011, with a team of powerful women, including Darshana's and Corinne's strong interest, I could finally resign from my full-time job. I told Dave that I was grateful for all he'd taught me and that I was now ready to get serious about my dream of launching a women's health company. He gave me his blessing, and the management team seemed equally supportive.

Now it was time to build our prototype. I signed a contract with Accel. We began to go back and forth on prototypes of a hydraulically propelled camera that would allow visualization of infertility-causing blockages. We realized that the camera didn't need to be pill-shaped if it was smooth enough not to damage the fallopian tube wall and could be propelled using saline. This was the first time I saw drawings sketched on the back of an envelope come to life.

Once we had a couple of prototypes, I wanted to show them to a physician or two to get their feedback. I reached out to Dr. Connor, who invited me to visit her in Florida and attend a minimally invasive gynecology conference she was helping to organize. She insisted I stay with her and her husband at their vacation home. We met in the lobby of the hotel in Fort Lauderdale where the conference was taking place, with million-dollar yachts idling by. After asking about my flight and if I needed anything to eat, she got down to business and introduced me to her boss and other big-name physicians attending the conference.

Later that evening, as we were sipping glasses of her favorite Chardonnay on her balcony, Dr. Conner and I chatted about the day's conference. The conversation eventually turned to what other diseases could be treated or diagnosed once a device was developed that could safely travel the length of the fallopian tube. We discussed one lecture from the conference that made the point that ovarian cancer is a misnomer. Instead, it should be called fallopian tube cancer because most ovarian cancers originate there. So far, we had been working on navigating and visualizing the fallopian tube. What if we could use everything we had learned to collect cells from the fallopian tube and examine them for unusual features, as is done with the Pap smear? Even in the hot, humid Florida air, a chill went down my spine. Could we develop a device to do just that? We were onto something.

As much as I wanted to drop everything and start working on the cell collection device, I had received funding to develop the imaging device that would look for blockages, and I felt like I had to see it through. I had been working with Accel on the imaging product for a few months before it was ready for more serious testing. Any medical- or health-related product takes a while to get to market and requires many steps of testing. First, researchers try to reproduce the anatomy in representative models to test medical device prototypes as best they can, often using store-bought pipes and other inorganic material. Next, they move on to testing with extracted animal tissue and then with live animals. Each of these milestones reduces the risk that the product won't work, without having to try it on human patients. When these steps are completed, the product will finally be safe enough for clinical studies.

We had reached the stage where we could show that we could hydraulically propel a camera through small, clear plastic tubing bent at different and increasingly complex angles. Testing the product in tissue—in other words, a piece of animal meat—was the next step in the process. I started reading about female animals' reproductive systems (uterus and fallopian tubes) that are similar to ours. It turns out that we are pretty unique in that particular way, even though many animals have similar hearts and digestive systems, for example. The closest animals are rabbits and sheep, but rabbit tubes are even smaller than ours, about half the size, and sheep have a septum that runs through the middle of their uterus, dividing it in two. I decided to try these options anyway.

We started with rabbit fallopian tubes. Accel had a medical-grade tissue source they worked with, and for $200, we got a single rabbit fallopian tube. But it was so small and unstructured that we couldn't manipulate it at all; in fact, we couldn't even find the opening! It just looked like a heap of guts on the lab bench. Next, we tried sheep fallopian tubes. We got a quote from the medical-grade tissue supplier and it was $1,000 for one. With only $250,000 raised, I didn't feel comfortable spending that kind of money on a single sample. We would have to go through dozens, if not hundreds of them, for testing. Tight budgets make you creative.

I thought to myself, *What if we had access to the tissue removed from the animals after they were slaughtered for another reason, like for meat consumption, and the parts were just going to be thrown out anyway?* I started calling livestock farms in California that sell lamb meat and found one a couple of hours north of my office. I asked if they would save some reproductive systems for me, and they said sure—for five dollars each. I made the drive to the farm myself and picked up ten. The smell on my drive back home made me wish I had remembered to bring a cooler. Luckily, after we took them out of the box and examined them, we discovered that they were usable.

As I had my head down, focused on the engineering side of things, yet another exciting email popped up from Anula. One of the venture capitalists she worked with, Tim Draper, was starting a new program for entrepreneurs, Draper University. Tim is a famed billionaire venture capitalist in his own right, investing in companies like Hotmail and the cryptocurrency Bitcoin, always thinking about the future. His father, William Henry Draper III, was one of the founders of venture capital in the country. The pilot program of Draper University would be six weeks long. I had fun filling out the application and gave it my all. Again, I saw the application as an opportunity to tell a great story. But I didn't expect to be accepted into the program. After being rejected by basically all the men I spoke to in Silicon Valley, why would one of its biggest names choose to take a chance on me?

We were in New York visiting Rajeev's sister when I got the acceptance email from Draper University. "This isn't just an acceptance letter," it read. "It's a call to action . . . That's what Draper University is all about—helping you become a super-hero, a change agent, the kind of entrepreneur who can defy the odds, solve big problems, and do nothing less than change the world." *This is so crazy*, I thought to myself. *This is so me.* I had to attend. That meant flying back a few days early from the trip to start the program.

I arrived late that first day, during Tim's introductory speech (classic Surbhi: I hadn't left enough time to find a parking spot). Tim stopped right in the middle of his speech, looked up at me, and said, "The next time you're going to be late, don't show up at all." Not the best first impression. As I scanned the room, I saw about thirty other entrepreneurs, a mix of men and women. At the time, I had no idea how close we would become. I would be a bridesmaid for one of them, Chrissy, a jewelry designer and owner of her own business, who would deck me out for my first magazine interview.

The curriculum at Draper University was a mix of traditional and nontraditional coursework. Tim brought in world-class speakers. He said the future was battery-operated cars, taking us to the Tesla factory for the very first viewing of the Model S before Tesla would become a household name. He told us about a newly emerging trend, something that could change the face of currency and the economy as we knew it—Bitcoin.

Now for the nontraditional part. We would jump into the pool with our clothes on. Tim would ask us to speak in front of the whole class without notice. In downtown San Mateo, we would go door to door, trying to sell store owners random things that Tim had selected, including, at one point, a vibrator. One afternoon, we gathered on the roof of a massive building Tim owned and tried to build contraptions to prevent an egg from breaking as we tossed it from a ten-story height. Why would Tim make us do these eccentric things? To get us comfortable in our skin. To become familiar with our boundaries and reach past them. It had the desired effect. Coming out of Draper University, hearing from all these outstanding entrepreneurs and having a better understanding of my capabilities, I felt like I could do anything.

The time at Draper University culminated in a pitch competition. One of the things that made me nervous about the event was that I would present a highly scientific product, while all the other companies participating in the program were tech- or internet-based. Not just that, but the investors coming to the competition would also have backgrounds investing mostly in software. I carefully thought through the message I wanted to convey and tried to simplify it as best I could: there was a significant unmet need in women's health, and I had the team and technological solution to address it.

Simplicity is vastly underrated. Entrepreneurs and other folks tend to believe that if they make their message sound complicated, others will think of them as an expert. Instead, investors might think that you are trying to pull the wool over their eyes. And if they don't "get" something, they aren't going to buy into it. For example, I could say that the fallopian tube is hard to navigate because of its thin wall thickness and tortuosity. Or I could say that it behaves like a light, wet paper towel. The first description sounds more scientific, but the second is easier for the audience to visualize and understand.

As we practiced pitching for the competition, Tim offered me a valuable piece of advice. From reading my application to Draper University, he knew that the seminal reason I went into women's health was because of my medical problems in high school. I didn't share this fact in previous pitches because I was afraid it would give the impression that I wasn't working on the device because I thought it was a large, profitable market, which investors want to hear, but for emotional reasons. I didn't want to come across as being someone who should run a nonprofit (not that there's anything wrong or trivial about that, but my aim was different).

Tim taught me I could do both: tell my story and make a business case. He encouraged me to open the pitch with my experiences as a young woman navigating my disease and the medical community and then hit the audience with the facts. He felt strongly that you could do good and make money, that these things are not mutually exclusive. I agreed to add my personal story to the pitch, even though it was hard for me to talk about. It was worth the trepidation, however, because it engaged the audience from the get-go. My vulnerability helped establish connection and empathy, which built rapport. I found that the more

I was willing to share experiences that relate to my overall message, the more likely people were to pay attention.

I won the pitch competition at the end of the program, and Tim offered me a chance to pitch to him—this time for real money. But in true Tim fashion, he approached me one morning and said, "Hey, can you pitch to me today at two p.m. for fifteen minutes?" The problem was, both Corinne and Darshana were already on flights to the Bay Area. They wanted to see for themselves if our product could actually capture an image in sheep fallopian tubes. I was supposed to meet them at 3:00 p.m. It was an especially important meeting—they were going to evaluate the progress of the prototype to see if they would invest the other $125,000. Tim couldn't make any other time. I decided I would pitch to him and then race from San Mateo to Los Gatos, some 45 minutes away, for my meeting with Darshana and Corinne.

Was pitching Tim really worth the risk of being late for Corinne and Darshana?

Tim decided to invest in me, and the sheep fallopian tube testing went well later that afternoon, so yes, it ended up being worth the risk. Tim was the very first man to believe in nVision. I soon came to learn that Tim often supported female entrepreneurs.

The additional investment brought our seed round from $250,000 to $500,000, allowing us to try a different design of the device and to do more testing on the prototypes than we had originally planned. I was worried that the hydraulic propulsion idea might not work in the fallopian tubes. Perhaps we wouldn't be able to get enough pressure to move the camera forward without damaging the fallopian tube, and the optical technology we were considering wasn't small enough. Now we had enough money to find out.

I researched what other companies had done to traverse the fallopian tube, at least the proximal portion of it, and found Imagyn in Irvine, California. Imagyn had tried to place what is called a linear everting balloon catheter (a balloon that unrolls like a tube sock) into the fallopian tube. The balloon would be gentle enough to traverse the tube, but could also be expanded, making it more rigid when entering the beginning of the fallopian tube, which is more muscular. I looked at the names of the original inventors of the technology, which was easy to do because the device, the Fogarty-Chin linear everting (unfolds from the inside out) balloon catheter, was named after its inventors. Dr. Albert Chin, or Al as he prefers to be called, is a prolific, well-respected physician turned inventor who happened to know both a former colleague of mine and Darshana. I sought a meeting with him through the company, which he agreed to. We met for the first time in September 2012. He thought it would be possible to get one of his linear everting balloons into the fallopian tube and then to place a camera through the balloon and image the tube through the clear wall of the balloon.

Al not only can produce high-level concepts and has over two hundred issued patents to his name, but he had the resources to create early prototypes of the balloon device. He first created some large-scale balloons to demonstrate the concept and then worked with another outsourced engineering shop to create smaller prototypes. Just a month after meeting with Al, we had a few early-stage prototypes with balloons that I could test in tissue.

We were able to take an image of the tube with both the new balloon concept as well as the propulsion concept I was working on with Accel. But it turned out that the sheep fallopian tubes weren't a good model in terms of demonstrating successful navigation (so good thing they only cost five bucks). The human fallopian tube starts with a very small inner diameter and grows larger as you traverse it: only about 1 millimeter at its opening, and ending at between 7 and 10 millimeters. The sheep fallopian tube is the opposite; it starts out large and as it progresses it becomes smaller and smaller. Though we could image the sheep fallopian tube and show some proof of concept, the model simply wasn't as representative as we wanted it to be.

I spoke to one of my advisors, who told me to talk to Dr. Jose Garza, a leading physician in Monterrey, Mexico, who had worked with several US-based medical device companies that were creating new products. In fact, almost any successful women's health medical device that has come to market in the last two decades has passed through his hands. Dr. Garza said that if we paid for his patients' already scheduled hysterectomies, he could then deliver us the uterus and fallopian tubes directly after they were excised, with their permission. This sounded like an excellent opportunity to see the device work in the right anatomy.

The only problem was this was happening in the year 2012, and Monterrey was overrun by drug cartels, who are not known for their interest in women's health initiatives. The consulting engineers of Accel demonstrated real dedication when they flew to Mexico with me for testing. The whole town felt deserted. Trucks full of soldiers holding massive guns lined the street. Few civilians were even driving in their cars. We established a routine that felt safe, eating only in the restaurant attached to the hotel, which was empty; using the deadlock bolt on our hotel doors at night; and always going directly from the airport to the operating room, to the hotel, to the operating room, and back to the airport on each trip. Even though the hotel had built an over-the-high-way walking ramp from its building to a neighboring mall, we were too scared to use it. Little did I know at the time, I would spend 2012 to 2016 going to Monterrey every few weeks, and that I would fall in love with the city.

Even after making the trip down, we couldn't get the hy-draulic propulsion prototype to work in the removed human uterus. The uterus and the proximal fallopian tubes are heavily vascularized; in other words, there is a lot of blood flow to the area. As soon as the uterus is removed from the body, blood flow stops, and the tissue almost immediately shrinks. This makes the fallopian tube outside the body even smaller than when it is inside the body. Given this small, restrictive opening, there just wasn't enough hydraulic propulsion to move the en-doscope through the fallopian tube. Luckily, we had better luck with Al's linear everting balloons and were able to take some good images of the tube.

When I spoke to Al, I shared with him the conversation I had had with Dr. Connor—that if we were able to retrieve cells from the fallopian tube, we could perhaps detect ovarian cancer. I had been considering how I would access those cells. One method would be to flush cells out of the fallopian tube using saline and then look at those cells for malignant features. This would require plugging the end of the fallopian tube so that the cells wouldn't just fall out the other end into the peritoneal cavity. He was inspired and, being the prolific inventor that he is he came up with numerous concepts to try to irrigate the fallopian tube.

At this point, I was working overtime and neglecting myself and my social life (and still not paying myself a salary, spending all of the money raised on testing). Dinner with some girlfriends was in order. I invited Opal and Mallika, my close friends from high school, and an ex-coworker, Bethany, to meet for Italian food in downtown Palo Alto. Mallika joined the dinner late, after we had consumed the first bottle of wine, so we of course had to order another bottle. My friends, the ones present at this dinner and otherwise, had been there for me since the start. Julia edited my business plan, Deborah sketched my first technical drawing of the catheter, and Aruna designed my first logo. I realized how lucky I was to have them. Not only did they readily forgive me for going MIA from time to time, but they supported me and reminded me that there was joy to be found outside of work.

The cherished friends at the table that night also knew I had started the company with cancer in mind, so they asked me how that aspect of the company was going. Right before meeting with them, I had read another academic paper ("Evaluation of DNA from the Papanicolaou Test to Detect Ovarian and Endometrial Cancers" — bedtime reading at its finest) out of the lab of famed researcher Bert Vogelstein. I was able to tell them a bit about it. The authors had succeeded in picking up some ovarian cancers by evaluating Pap smear samples from the cervix using their new molecular test. The paper indicated that the test would have even greater accuracy if cells from the fallopian tube could be analyzed.

After dinner, I found myself in the back of a cab to San Francisco, still thinking about the research paper. My thoughts also went to my grandmother. I was happy that we were making progress and believed that we were solving a needed clinical indication, but since high school, it had always been ovarian cancer that I wanted to work on. As I stretched in the backseat of the car, a thought occurred to me: *What if we could use the surface of the balloon itself to retrieve cells?* It wouldn't damage the anatomy, or add any more steps or complexity to the procedure. You could then dip the balloon in some cell preservation fluid, just as they do for the Pap smear, and look for malignant features of the cell.

I emailed Al Chin the next day. "Another thing to add to our patent," I wrote. "There is a chance that aspiration/flushing may not exert enough force on the lumen wall to shake enough cancerous cells loose. In this case, we would need a cytology brush in the fallopian tube to collect a sample. However, we may not have room for that. I think we should use a linear everting balloon that is heavily textured, to have the same effect as a brush." I didn't know it at the time, but this would be the eventual product that nVision worked on, after a tremendous amount of iteration and refinement from Al and other engineers who joined the team; it marked the beginning of our ultimate device.

With the progress that we had made, I decided it was time to raise our next round of funding to accelerate our efforts. I was hoping to raise $4 million, with the goal of this round being to obtain some clinical data and FDA clearance.

Darshana and her fund decided to lead the round, putting $2.5 million on the table. All I had to do was fill in the rest. But it was the same thing as last time, rejection after rejection. Anula then introduced me to Astia, an organization founded in 1999 in Silicon Valley focused on investing in innovative startups led by women. Sharon Vosmek is the CEO and an early-stage investor with a track record of working with female entrepreneurs. Astia has since launched a venture capital fund but back then managed a group of angel investors who would invest money into companies that they liked.

So now, I stepped onstage in front of a huge conference room at DLA Piper, a law firm based in Palo Alto. DLA Piper offered legal advice to Astia but also offered its space to them for investor meetings. For my presentation, there were about fifty Astia angels present. I was competing (as least it felt like that to me) with two other female entrepreneurs, who seemed very impressive. I started presenting and at some point, like I always do, said a very intimidating word: *VAGINA*. The men had reactions that I had become all too familiar with: some leaned in with eyes wide open (*Maybe I'll see one!*), some cringed and leaned back (*Maybe I'll see one!*). Eventually, I found that the word *transvaginal* made male investors more comfortable, so I changed my pitch. Today I probably wouldn't, but then, as a first-time entrepreneur doing whatever I had to in order to get the company off the ground, I felt it was a wise decision.

It's incredibly important to know the background of the audience you plan on speaking to so that you can assess their personalities and predict the way they could react to each element of your story. And you should know your story so well that you can change what you are emphasizing on the fly, based on facial expressions and body language you observe in the moment, not just questions.

I left the room to allow the Astia angel investors to discuss the opportunity among themselves. Karen and Anula were in the room, and I learned from them that the discussion was quite animated—some folks struggle to see that women's health isn't a small market, even if it does impact half the population. Fortunately, the room was filled with both male and female investors, which is unusual for early-stage investment groups. As a result, Astia came through with more than a million dollars of investment including checks from some of the partners at DLA Piper. I did not know at the time that nVision would become Astia's first investment and go on to become their most successful exit from the original portfolio, enabling them to go on to raise their first venture fund.

With Darshana's $2.5 million and the $1 million from Astia, I had only $500,000 left to reach my goal of raising $4 million. I presented to another angel group, Life Science Angels, and they agreed to invest after I had pitched them at a dinner meeting, during which I was introduced to the only other woman entrepreneur there, Erika Stanzl (she became and remains a close friend). My champion at Life Science Angels, Faz Bashi, thought that I should set up a meeting with the Berkeley Angel Network as well. But the Berkeley Angel Network met only once a month, and by the time the meeting with them rolled around, we had raised our full $4 million and there was no room for them. I explained this to the organizer, and though she was annoyed that I would waste everyone's time, she asked me to present anyway. I went onstage and told the room full of people that there wasn't any more availability in the round before telling the nVision story. The number of people interested in nVision broke their

previous record (people always want what they can't have—
FOMO is real). I accommodated them by increasing my round
size to $4.5 million, even though raising more money meant that
I had to give up more ownership of my company.

With a total of $4.5 million in our second fundraising round,
money was starting to burn a hole in my pocket. It was time for
me to hire a team that would get us through our first human
studies and earn FDA clearance. We were making great progress with consultants, but until you have people who are thinking
only about your product, progress is capped. Outside manufacturing firms and consultants have hundreds of different clients
that they are working with. I wanted people to obsess over the
exact product design we needed the same way I was. Now was
the time to find them.

5

La Familia

Building a Team That Lasts

On one especially hot, muggy Mexican summer day in 2014, Jesus Magaña along with other members of the nVision team and I were crammed into a small, rectangular office room with no windows and no air-conditioning. A fan, constantly running in the background, was working overtime to keep us cool. Neither the sweltering heat nor the humming of the fan bothered us; we were grateful for the opportunity to work with one of the premier research-oriented hospitals in Mexico, Universidad Autónoma de Nuevo León, for our first clinical study. We readily accepted any space offered to gather and decompress between clinical cases.

Despite my hopes, after two years, there were still no direct flights from San Francisco to Monterrey, where the hospital was. Because we were a small team on a tight budget, we often opted for overnight journeys, going straight from the airport to the hospital just in time for the first case, usually scheduled for 8:00 a.m.—or 7:00 a.m. in our time zone in California. We were working around the clock, but at least we were able to catch the sunrise, which turned the jagged, imposing mountains red. I looked around at the exhausted team and felt both awe and appreciation that they had, yet again, been willing to take the overnight flight and eat soggy plane eggs to be here with me.

On this particular morning, the first clinical case of the day had not gone as well as expected. No harm to the patient, but our balloon catheter didn't deploy like we wanted it to. We were brainstorming what we could do differently in the next case when Dr. Garza entered the office. He can command any room with his larger-than-life presence, and his tales always captured our attention. Between cases, he would regale us with epic stories about his travels around the world or impress us with the background stories on his breakthrough inventions. On this day, he decided to share a personal tale about obtaining the watch on his wrist, a limited-edition Rolex Oyster Mickey Mouse, one of the most prized pieces in his massive Rolex collection.

After he left the room, I noticed the usually jovial Jesus looking a little down. When I asked him what was wrong, he said, "You know, Surbhi, I've worked as hard as possible my entire life. I love watches, but not only will I never be able to wear a Rolex, I won't be able to afford to send my three kids to college." At that moment, I choked out a promise to him: if he stuck with me, he would indeed be able to send his kids to school, and I would buy him that Rolex.

I'm not sure what Jesus thought of my promise at the moment. Succeeding enough for me to buy a fancy watch or fund college tuition probably seemed as unlikely as it was for us all to be in that room together, trying to get clinical data for a medical device that might change women's health.

Though we were in Jesus's native country, we were both literally and figuratively far from where his story started. Jesus was born in a small village where he remembers having to fight off scorpions and rattlesnakes, and often depended on fish in the nearby river for dinner. He recalls his father as aloof and his mother as warm. One day when he was still a small boy, she fell gravely ill. It turned out to be cancer, but she passed away before the doctors of the village had figured out the type. He remembers her bloating and discomfort, both signs of ovarian cancer, and now, as an adult, often wonders if that's what she was suffering from.

His mother's death eventually led Jesus to crossing the border into the US illegally, alone, when he was eleven years old. He found his way to San Francisco, where his distant family members lived. He started going to school but was unable to keep up with the classwork since he didn't speak much English. He was also exhausted. Expected to earn his keep to stay with extended family who couldn't afford another mouth to feed, he picked up jobs during the day and also worked at night, cleaning up at local bars and often falling asleep on the hard floors at 3:00 a.m. Jesus's determination didn't keep him on those bar floors for long.

Who could be more doubted than this little boy? But this is the story of so many immigrants, of so many people! If you work hard and have a bit of luck, unimaginable things can happen.

Other people will see your value, and it'll help you see your own value. Even without ever attending high school, Jesus's natural talent and work ethic allowed him to advance from odd jobs to a steady income assembling products on manufacturing lines at medical device companies. He wasn't expected to be creative in that job, he was only required to put together products based on the written instructions placed in front of him. Still, he couldn't help but see improvements that could be made to existing designs or come up with more efficient manufacturing steps, and never hesitated to point them out. His superiors took notice, and he was promoted to technician.

Decades later, through a connection with a mutual colleague, I met Jesus and hired him as an R&D technician. He advanced and enhanced the design of our device, but he also did something more. He held us together and he even gave a name to what we were to each other: La Familia.

When I set out to create a company, if someone told me that the best part would be the people and the culture we created together, I wouldn't have believed them. After all, what could top seeing a concept scribbled on the back of a napkin come to life as a prototype? Or watching an idea evolve into a fully functioning device that works in people? But it is true — building and working with the nVision team was more rewarding than the first check we got from an investor. It was even more gratifying than our company's acquisition.

Hiring the right team is one of the topics I get asked about most from new founders and new managers. Rightfully so, since it's the most make-or-break aspect of any project. How do you go about making sure that you're hiring the person with the appropriate technical or operational background? Who also has the right mind-set and attitude? Finding the balance of experience and values is not an easy task. Furthermore, how do you make sure that the people you bring on will mesh with and enhance the culture you want to craft? It can be a surprisingly difficult, all-consuming experience if you hire the wrong person. The flipside to this, of course—and the opportunity—is that finding the right person can lead to magic. When I first started hiring our full-time team, I was tempted to hire anyone with medical device experience so I could offload some of the various items on my plate. When you have an overwhelming amount of work, it's easy to fall into the trap of hiring the first person willing to take the job. Some people resort to seeing which one of their friends is available and then evaluating if there is any work at the company that this friend could tackle. Though your immediate network is a great place to start recruiting, your friends may not be the most qualified people for the particular jobs you need to fill—and you need to get the best person possible. That's why I advise founders and leaders to flip the script and do things the other way around. To me, the first step is not to think about who you know, but what you need. In other words, think through the milestones you are driving toward. Then, think about the type of people you want in your corner to accomplish those specific goals. What kind of experience and skills do you want these people to have? Once you start creating these ideal profiles, it's easier to understand the kinds of people who might be a good fit.

In addition to the operational experience that you're looking for, it's never too early to think about the cultural values you want your company to have. Discovering this means getting together with your cofounders or early employees and having an open discussion about what's important to them—what type of environment do they want to create that will make them look forward to coming into the office every day? For nVision, most of our team gravitated to the company because of the potential impact the product could have on patients. We also had a mantra to take work seriously, but not ourselves. No need to follow a dress code or avoid self-deprecating humor. We wanted people who didn't block others' progress and, therefore, respected other people's time. Deadlines were never just for show. The cultural values I wanted to build not only centered around alignment of goals, mutual respect, tenacity, empathy, and the love of hard work but also working smart and being down to earth.

A company culture happens by design or default. If you aren't deliberate about the type of people you want to hire and the culture you want to build together, you will still have a culture—it just might not be the one you want. Establishing values is a personal call—do what feels right to you, what feels natural—and your cultural beliefs will help to establish a day-to-day experience that employees look forward to and that will help keep people together when things get rough. If you start with an objective list of experiences that you're looking for, as well as a written list of cultural values, you are less likely to fall victim to your own inherent bias. Such clarity is the best insurance against hiring someone whom you think you would enjoy hanging out with, instead of someone who can get the job done. Remember: you are hiring to achieve a particular goal. People who have the type of skills that you need can come from any socioeconomic background, any generation, any race or gender. If we didn't think someone was a good fit, we always tried to articulate out loud why. If one can't quite say, that might be an unknown bias creeping into the equation when it shouldn't. Because I saw diversity as a value and kept an open mind, and remembered not to underrate those with different backgrounds, my first four hires were a Chinese American in his sixties, a Caucasian man in his fifties, a woman engineer in her twenties, and Jesus, who, in this incarnation, was a Mexican American in his forties without a high school diploma.

Though in hindsight it may have been a mistake, nVision began with the concept to stay "virtual" for as long as possible. Before the time of the pandemic and the prevalence of Zoom, that meant not having an office space and relying heavily on phone calls and consultants. I powered through all of the work with a part-time team because I wanted to make the money last as long as possible and didn't take a single cent for granted. Although the newly raised $4.5 million was available, I wasn't ready to hire a full-time team until I was sure that we had a concept that worked. I was worried that if I hired a bunch of people, I wouldn't be able to control the spend. Once you hire someone, you have to pay for their salary, even if things go wrong or you aren't making as much progress as expected. When it's just you and something goes amiss, you can hit the pause button and not have the responsibility of meeting payroll. I do not, however, recommend working with consultants for as long as I did (a full eighteen months). As I said earlier, people who are working on something full time typically care more.

Our core tasks at nVision were to finalize the design of the product, build and test the product as much as possible before animal or human testing, move on to human clinical studies, and finally, apply for FDA approval. To do this, I would need engineers with a variety of skill sets: someone who could come up with the high-level concept/innovation; someone who could translate that into an early-stage prototype and also navigate the regulatory requirements of creating the necessary supporting documentation; and a technician who could enhance the design and build several iterations of the devices for testing.

From my first round of funding, which closed in January 2012, all the way until June 2013, there was no other full-time person on the team besides me. While it was not that productive (or fun) to work alone, the task of finding a full-time technical team was daunting. I had faced a great deal of rejection when looking for other engineers to start the company with me. Startup founders know that they're pitching when they raise capital, or when they present in front of executive teams, but they often don't realize they always have to be pitching. This is especially true with recruiting and hiring. Whether you're interviewing an engineer fresh out of school or a pro with decades of experience under their belt, think of every candidate as having a vast amount of opportunity. You have to sell them on yours. Why would they choose you and your company?

As I thought about the work we needed to get done and the potential candidates who would be capable, it occurred to me that Dave Snow, my old boss, had left his last full-time position and was consulting. He had exactly the type of experience I needed; he had gotten a dozen products, if not more, through to FDA approval. Imagine his surprise, and frankly, mine, when we were again sitting across the table, but this time I was the one asking him questions. It isn't an easy task to convince your ex-boss to now be your employee.

We shared an especially tasty meal at a new fast-food French place in downtown San Carlos, where Dave lived. In truth, the nVision opportunity wasn't a slam dunk for Dave. He had found his stride consulting for different startups and was enjoying the variety of clients and their challenges. With two young children at home, the flexibility of his schedule was a major plus. I was also a first-time entrepreneur and CEO, and Dave, with numerous successful company acquisitions under his belt, could have worked anywhere. He ultimately agreed to do some consulting work on a part-time basis. This would give him an opportunity to see what reporting to me might feel like.

Dave mentioned that while I worked for him, he could tell that I gave the job everything that I had and was a fast learner, even when he and other leaders of the company gave me more responsibilities. Reputation is incredibly important in the professional and corporate world. Because I excelled at new challenges, he felt confident that I would work hard to learn how to be a CEO, a job that is vastly different from that of an engineer.

I believe another reason Dave was compelled to join was that though we hadn't done a great job keeping in touch in the two years since I left the job working for him, we still felt close. Just as important as having hard technical talent is the softer side of things. I had played with his girls when they came into the office, and Dave supported me through the loss of my grand-mother and my dog Panther.

As an aside, I understand that it can feel difficult to open up to others in a professional setting. It's even harder to share when you have doubters, or you're worried about the existence of bias. The chances that someone might judge you for something that's out of your control are much higher. People who are seen as "other" may have more trouble opening up in a professional setting because colleagues might not relate to them personally. Consider if you're an all-American family that watches football together on Sunday, and a lot of your colleagues are the same, then you bond over some commonalities. But if your normal weekend routine includes going to Indian dance practice or taking classes in your family's native language, then maybe you feel a bit less comfortable sharing because it's less of a connection point. As with everything, you need to find the line that makes you feel comfortable.

Overall, the more that you ask about your coworkers' lives and the more you're willing to share yours (when appropriate), the more of a human connection you form. Nothing persists through time and memory like human connection. You might leave your job and go through a stretch of silence that lasts years, but you'll greet each other with a smile when you finally run into one another. Dave and I come from different religious backgrounds, different generations, and have different interests, but because we respect and care for each other, we transcended those differences and formed a strong lifelong bond.

While I was elated that Dave agreed to spend half his time with nVision, and energized that our core team was growing, we were having trouble with the development of the product, specifically the optical components of the device. The vendor in Germany that supplied us with cameras repeatedly missed deadlines, as the size of camera we required necessitated additional and unforeseen research and development on their part. Instead of waiting on them, I decided to spend R&D resources on the idea I couldn't stop thinking about—a device that would collect cells from the fallopian tube, which would enable the detection of ovarian cancer. We wouldn't be starting from scratch; if things went according to plan, we would be able to utilize the same balloon technology. Instead of putting a camera through the balloon, we would use the surface of the balloon to collect cells. I wasn't aware of it then because it was a side project, but I was actually pivoting the company away from the original idea of detecting blockages in the fallopian tube. I didn't know if this idea would develop into anything. but I did know that anything forward moving is better than standing still.

A lot of entrepreneurs are afraid to pivot—after all, working on something brand-new is a big deal, especially when you have investors on board that supported the original idea. I wasn't building a company for the sake of building a company, though. I was in a hurry to help patients. If one idea was stalling, and I wasn't sure if it was going to work, I was going to try something else, especially if I had a chance to work on ovarian cancer. Plus, I was leveraging what I knew about navigating the fallopian tube for a new application, so all of the past effort wasn't a waste.

This caused considerable disagreement at the board level. Darshana had invested in a device that could detect fallopian tube blockages, and pivoting to detecting ovarian cancer, a much more complex market, didn't sit well with her. Needless to say, it's a very big deal to misdiagnose cancer, and though billions of dollars had been spent on early detection of ovarian cancer, no one had found a way to do it successfully. What were the chances we could?

Anula and Corinne, on the other hand, did want to explore the opportunity, and eventually Darshana came around to spending some money on exploring options for a cell collection device. But our different perspectives on this issue continued to be challenging. It was at this time that Darshana and I had our first full-blown argument. I inappropriately rolled my eyes when she objected to further spending on R&D for the cell collection device. After the meeting, she pulled me aside and reminded me that we were in a marriage, that we were going to see through our differences together, one way or another, and that every marriage has its hard years. Eventually, we overcame our differences and came to an agreement. I would hire a marketing consultant to look into the opportunity and market size for the ovarian cancer device if she agreed to let us spend money on R&D for it. Corinne and Anula were on board, so reluctantly Darshana agreed. After all, we all knew that detecting ovarian cancer early would solve an even more important unmet clinical need. It could save lives.

But if we were going to work on this, the investors wanted to see results—and fast.

As far as we could tell, no one had pursued this idea to use the surface of the balloon to collect cells. We first needed to test if it was even feasible. I drove up to the sheep farm yet again, and right before the July 4 weekend in 2013, we deployed our balloon into sheep tissue. We withdrew the balloon and smeared the sample we collected onto a slide. It was hard to control the floppy balloon without touching it and causing contamination. Once we looked at the slide under the microscope, we saw that we hadn't collected anything, so we knew we had to try another method.

On the next try, after deploying the balloon, we cut it off from our device and put it into cytopreservative, a fluid that's used for transporting and storing cells. Our hope was that the liquid would preserve any cells collected on the surface of the balloon. Once that was done, we needed an expert to analyze the slide and tell us if we had actually captured any cells.

Al knew a pathologist from a previous job and connected me to him. I dropped off the slides directly to his home in the San Bruno hills, where he had a makeshift lab set up for his side hustle. The most seminal of inventions can happen in the most casual of places. The next day he emailed me: "Here is good news. For an initial run, I stained a smear made from one of the test tubes. The smear had clusters of what looked like epithelial cells. This is a good start." He sent us pictures of the cell samples we took, and there were plenty of them, and they looked intact. Incredible.

Whenever something works in an animal model, it's exciting. But we also knew that animal models don't always translate to working in a human. We wanted to test in human tissue as quickly as possible. I called Dr. Garza, and he agreed to do a study for us that September. He arranged for us to conduct studies on three different uteruses right after they were removed from the patient. Though there was too much tissue atrophy to test visualization of the tube, maybe we could still collect cells. We had two objectives we were assessing this study: (1) were we able to access the full length of the fallopian tube, and (2) were we able to collect enough cells?

We weren't able to do either. First, we couldn't access the fallopian tube because the balloon portion of our catheter was too big and too weak to pass through the muscular transition between it and the uterus. If the balloon was greater than 1 millimeter in outer diameter, it expanded the fallopian tube too much. The couple of times that we did manage to get the balloon into the fallopian tube, we weren't able to collect enough cells. Perhaps it was because Dr. Garza's lab required us to smear the cells from the balloon directly onto a slide, a method we knew didn't work from our sheep studies. A much worse possibility was that the balloon was able to pick up sheep cells, but not human cells for yet unknown reasons.

Later that month, I had another board meeting where I asked for additional funding to put toward the cell collection device. Given our subpar results and Darshana's continued hesitation, we had a contentious conversation. Since our optical components from Germany continued to be delayed, our options were to work on cell collection or do nothing. Somewhat reluctantly, the board agreed to spend more resources on cell collection.

If we kept on having failure after failure like this, I didn't know if the board would let me keep the position of CEO. After all, many early-stage founders are replaced by more "professional" CEOs the investor knows. I tried to put the board out of mind and focus on the team and the work ahead. This was a time of stress and uncertainty, but I've found that working on something really hard can bring people together. The right team will be drawn to and rally around a challenge. People want to feel like they are working on something that hasn't been done before, a problem that hasn't been solved—which can drive incredible results.

Even though the last study had not gone as smoothly as we

had hoped, we didn't lose our drive. We still believed we were onto something and scheduled more studies in Mexico in October. Dave, Al, and I had worked overtime in the seven weeks between studies. We were laser focused on improving the device based on what we learned from the prior study, and the results were remarkable. We reduced the diameter of the catheter down to 1 millimeter and added strength to the end of our device. We also added monofilament, similar to a piece of fishing line, to the end of our balloon, so there would be another part of the device besides the balloon making contact with the walls of the fallopian tube. With these changes in place, we were now able to access almost every fallopian tube we tested. Next, we attempted to enhance the preservation method in two ways: by smearing the cells onto slides and then leaving those behind with Dr. Garza's lab, and by cutting the balloons off our device and putting them into a vial with cytopreservative to bring them back to the US for our new consulting pathologist to look at.

We were incredibly fortunate to be working with Dr. Sharmila Pramanik as our pathology consultant. I had become friends with her son, Abhik, at UC Berkeley and one night, in a rare moment when I escaped the office for dinner, I was honest with him about all of the challenges we were facing at nVision. Abhik is in tech so he didn't really know what to do but thought that his mother, a well-known pathologist in the Bay Area, might be able to help. He made the introduction, and she graciously invited me to visit her in her office. I immediately noticed that she was friendly to everyone we ran into and they all responded in a deferential manner. It was obvious she was highly respected.

She made the time to listen to my ideas for the medical

device, as well as what to do with the cell sample we collected. Because she saw the promise of the idea and thought it was an issue worth solving, she was willing to go one step past discussion and also read the results of slides we brought to her after studies. Eventually, she did much more than that—she innovated along with us. She offered key advice about what the main features of the cell sample should be, and what to watch out for when developing the device. It wasn't just about how many cells you could collect, but the condition of those cells after they were collected.

Case in point: We gave Dr. Garza's lab and Dr. Pramanik samples from the same study. Again, the hospital lab in Monterrey found almost no cells. Dr. Pramanik used a different method to prep the samples, and her results told a different story: "They all have good cellularity in terms of volume, cell preservation, and cytology," she said. It was a eureka moment—it was possible to collect cells from human fallopian tubes using a balloon. Even with the long, complicated road ahead of us, the road that all cancer-related products have to go down, the entire board was finally convinced that we should spend more time and money on the cell collection device.

We still had work to do; it wouldn't be good enough to "almost always" access the tube. We needed to be even better every time. And with all these people on my side—bound together by a human connection to one another and a connection to the cause—I knew that we could.

Between September 2013 and March 2014, we went to Mexico every month for a study. Dave, Al, and I were worn out by the exhausting pace but making steady progress. Our access rate was at about 75 percent. In March, Dr. Garza offered a radical suggestion. He thought that our lower access rate of the fallopian tubes was caused by the fact that the tissue changed as soon as it was removed from the body. There were no ligaments or blood flow holding the fallopian tubes and uterus in position, so they collapsed, making them harder to navigate. He suggested we do a study in a patient directly before having a hysterectomy. Any part of the anatomy the device touched would be removed anyway, so the risk to the patient was relatively low.

Everything was about to get even more intense. If we were going to go into live humans, we would need to be even more ready and more certain. We'd also need to hire more people. Al moved from hourly work to signing a retainer for a set number of hours a week to guarantee his time. After a few months of consulting and working closely with Al, Dave was ready to join full time. But we would need even more engineering horsepower. In health care, designing the product is only half the battle. Documenting what the device looks like, what the specifications are, and what the risks are is also of paramount importance. This documentation is usually maintained by the engineering team as well as a group called quality. The quality department makes sure that the documentation and necessary testing is compliant with FDA requirements, and being done to a certain standard, which are essential to have in place before conducting clinical studies.

Finding someone to help us navigate this would not be easy. But it was critical to start searching. I began reaching out to my network from Abbott Vascular and reconnected with a female engineer named Brenna Hearn. With dual degrees from Stanford, she is wicked smart. Not only that, but she has a cheerful demeanor, something I had learned when I got to know her socially while at Abbott. If anyone had any complaints about her, it was that she could be "exacting." For us, that wasn't a flaw; it was a feature. Brenna agreed to consult with us, which she appreciated because it gave her the flexibility she needed to be around for pickup and drop-off at her kid's school.

I was thrilled to be working with one of the talented female engineers whom I started my career with, and Brenna's work did not disappoint. She had to generate hundreds of pages of documentation in a matter of weeks, and she did, with all details carefully spelled out, recording every specification of the device, component by component. When it was time to actually build devices for the clinical study, she had no qualms about donning a gown and cap and jumping into the clean room to participate in the hands-on work of building the device, carefully attaching miniscule pieces of material together to create our catheter. In part because of her effort, by April, we had built a human-ready device.

I also looked for resources on the quality side of things. We were introduced to Wendy Heigel, a scientist by training who had become a seasoned leader in the quality space. It took me a couple of emails to get a hold of her since she already had more clients than she could handle. I finally caught her between meetings and set up a time to sit down and talk. Wendy is a couple of inches shorter than me and had long, brown bangs that framed her face; she looked kind but intense. I pitched her the project we were working on. I could tell that she was intrigued so I made the ask we needed, which even I knew was seemingly impossible—would she be able to deliver us a design review of our product in four days so we could get into a clinical study the following month? It was a Friday, which meant she would have to work through the weekend. To our surprise, she agreed, and even more surprisingly, despite the daunting task, she delivered.

Wendy eventually became my right-hand person at nVision. When I was out of the office, the team looked to her for direction. I came to trust her implicitly. She eventually gave up her lucrative consulting gig to join me full time. This coup goes back to clearly articulating your vision and demonstrating that you have the drive and focus to achieve your goals. Attracting A-grade talent like Dave and Wendy had a positive, amplifying effect. Dave and Wendy joining helped other executives with impressive backgrounds feel comfortable coming aboard a ship steered by a young, first-time CEO.

Wendy worked so hard that if she left the office before 7:00 p.m., everyone would notice—and she only did that once every three months to get a haircut, her bangs being as precise as her documentation work. While her husband, Doug, is also a high-achieving professional in the medical device space, he would spend his personal time biking and working on his own small airplane. Wendy, on the other hand, is like me—she loves to work, preferring it to hobbies. The exception to this is that we would both watch *Game of Thrones* on weekends, discussing the latest plot developments with the team come Monday. Even though she is a workaholic, she is still human and open, so we were able to connect. Everyone enjoyed working for and with Wendy, and I liked having her report to me. She is a reliable operator and a relatable leader, which helped form both trust and bonds. If people know that you'll be there, it makes them much more likely to deliver—and that's exactly what we saw with our *familia*.

In May 2014, after years of thinking through the design, doing much experimentation, and building out a full team, we were ready to try the device in humans with their consent. As I stood with Dave and Al in the Monterrey operating room, covered in head-to-toe PPE, my heart was pounding. The physician placed our device at the opening of the fallopian tube and tried to deploy the balloon. We could see the balloon extending from the tip of our catheter, but it simply wasn't able to cross into the opening of the fallopian tube. That area of the body is too muscular, and the balloon wasn't strong enough. We had spent months and months of fourteen-hour days to get here, and we couldn't even make it into the fallopian tube. The doctor suggested that we try the other side. We held our breath and crossed our fingers, but the same thing happened. When we started to unfurl the balloon out of the tip of the catheter, it simply wouldn't enter the fallopian tube. It turned out that the opening is more muscular than the rest of the fallopian tube because it is found within the thick wall of the uterus.

We took a break before attempting the procedure on the next subject. There would be three subjects total in this study, so we had two more chances to get it right. Al, Dave, and I brainstormed what we could do differently. We couldn't change the device itself, but perhaps we could change the way we used it— perhaps we would have better luck entering the muscular opening of the fallopian tube with something stiffer. Instead of trying to unfurl the balloon directly into the fallopian tube, I thought that pre-deploying 2 centimeters of the balloon before it entered would allow the physician to guide that portion into the anatomy. We could also control the stiffness of the balloon by increasing the pressure we used to inflate it, so we took it up just a notch. We had already demonstrated that the balloon could withstand the pressure.

Al and Dave balked at the idea. They didn't think it would make any difference and that we would be wasting our time and the physician's. But I had a hunch about it, and wanted to try it.

We talked through the idea with the doctor, and he was equally hesitant to try it but willing because there would be no increased risk to the patient. We marked up the necessary changes in the Instruction for Use documentation and protocol, put on our PPE, and headed back into the operating room. The physician deployed 2 centimeters of the balloon, and I'm sure I looked like a deer in headlights as he tried to gently guide it into the fallopian tube. Success! Deploying a little bit of the balloon first provided the stiffness we needed to enter, and then gave the necessary direction to the rest. We were also able to navigate the patient's other fallopian tube successfully, as well as both fallopian tubes of the third patient. In terms of navigation, it was truly a huge success for our first attempt.

It was a reminder for me to pay attention to my own gut, even when experienced voices in the room disagreed. From then on, I continued to carefully listen to what others had to say, but took my own intuition equally seriously.

We took the cell samples we managed to collect back to the US to be analyzed by Dr. Pramanik. We waited a few long days for the results. Who cares if we could navigate the fallopian tube if we weren't able to grab any cells along the way? Unfortunately, that's what happened. It wasn't that we didn't grab enough cells; we did not collect any cells at all. The pathologist was confused. If we had made any contact with the fallopian tube, there should be at least some cells in one of the samples. Then it dawned on me. In order to get through the uterus with a hysteroscope, you have to distend the uterus with saline. When we tried to withdraw the balloon from the fallopian tube, it would enter the saline-filled uterus and the cells would be washed away. We would need to figure out a way to protect the cells.

Thanks to the tireless efforts of the team, and the collaborative way we worked with one another, six weeks later we returned with a new, improved design. We had added a sheath, a separate piece of tubing that the balloon was pulled into, protecting it from the environment, therefore preventing the cells on the balloon from being washed away. We also made some size and material changes to the balloon itself. The results were fantastic—not only were we able to navigate the fallopian tube, but we were able to pick up viable cells.

This was after months of trying, with failure after failure. This time, it wasn't just my good indignation that kept us going, it was our indignation now. We knew the clinical problem we were working on was worth however many iterations it took.

I felt like we were very close to what the final design might look like, but we needed certain experts to ensure we would get there. When it comes to medical device design, the 80/20 rule applies—we knew the last 20 percent of the design would be the hardest to finalize. My original hydraulic pill idea was completely out as we could never get it to work. Even for the infertility device, we had pivoted completely to placing an endoscope through

Al's balloon innovation. Working with such small components and putting them together in a consistent, repeatable way would be tricky. The next step would be to hire an R&D technician who could help us finalize the device design—and turn the prototypes that we were building into something that would scale production. Often, medical device technicians don't have a college degree, but have instead what we call "magical hands." They're able to assemble prototypes that college-educated engineers can only dream of building.

That's when Jesus, the person responsible for turning nVision into La Familia, first entered the picture. I reached out to see if anyone in my network knew of the perfect technician for our catheter-based device, and I was sent his name again and again. Jesus and I had worked at Abbott at the same time but never really crossed paths. I made a few calls to former colleagues and heard nothing but glowing reviews. Still, I was nervous about this hire, as it would be our first full-time employee. At this point, Al was on a monthly retainer but continued to work on other projects, and Dave was slowly making his way to joining full time but hadn't yet pulled the trigger.

We hired Jesus almost immediately, and it turned out to be one of the best decisions we made at nVision. His amazing technical skill set was only half of what he offered, because he also became the heart and soul of our company—he was unguarded, loyal—and when others might have held their tongue with me, he did not.

While things went well with Jesus and Dave, I made plenty of hiring mistakes along the way. For example, while still doing work for us, a consultant had interviewed for another role at a company working on balloon technology and accidently let one of our manufacturing secrets slip. This was a problem because our consulting agreement specifically stated that she could not disclose technical details of the company. This made its way not only back to me, but to my board. I was livid. A trade secret of ours had made it to another company? It was the first time I had to let someone go. It was devastating for both of us. In retrospect, maybe I should have given such a talented, hardworking female engineer the benefit of the doubt. She hadn't done anything maliciously. But that's the problem with letting someone go—you have to first weigh all of the facts and then go with what you know at the time without having any guarantee that it's the right decision. The vast majority of the time it is, not only for the company, but for the person you are letting go.

To make sure we didn't have individual bias creeping into decisions to let someone go, we made a habit of always discussing the decision extensively as a group. And again, we asked one another to articulate out loud what the issues were and would carefully document them as well.

That wasn't the only misstep we had with a team member. One of the candidates we ended up hiring for a clinical role had used the word *hoo-ha* to describe the vagina, not once, but over and over and over again during interviews. Weirder yet, he didn't use the term because women's health was new to him; he had worked in the space for several years. We're in the health care field, so a certain level of professionalism and comfort with anatomy is expected. I still can't believe that the team and I ignored this red flag and brought him on full time. Our previous hire for this role had left us suddenly to pursue another company with much more funding, right before the start of a clinical study, and we were desperate to replace her—a little too desperate. We should have taken the warning signs from the interview seriously, as the *hoo-ha* candidate turned out to be less than professional in other ways once he got the full-time job.

In another instance, a candidate lied to us during the interview process. She said she was the one who had made the decision to leave her last company, when in fact she had been fired. I only found out the truth when speaking to a reference she provided in the application process. I confronted her, and she apologized, and again the team decided to move forward because we had a big deadline coming up. Neither of these hiring decisions worked out and ultimately ended up delaying us. Don't ignore red flags.

This can be hard to do; certain positions can be incredibly difficult to hire for because candidates are scarce. Sometimes that can breed desperation, especially when you're running a venture-backed company where investors are pleased to see you build a big team and expect a certain amount of growth. But don't let that cloud your judgment and influence your decisions. Wrong hires made quickly can do more damage and set you back further than taking more time to find the right person.

Though proceeding with caution during the hiring process is important, there is no way to learn everything you need to know about a person during the one or two hours you spend with them. So eventually, no matter how good a job you and your team do with the hiring process, you'll end up with limited data. As a result, you will, at some point, be faced with having to let someone go. The first couple of times that I had to do this, it was incredibly difficult. Many first-time CEOs and new managers report the same challenge. You always doubt yourself because most candidates do something right, so you can point to their strengths and ignore their weaknesses. But someone's weaknesses can lead to the destruction of your company and your team during those crucial early stages. Do the math: if you are a ten-person team, one person makes up 10 percent of your culture and your workforce. When you make the call and let the wrong hire go, something happens almost instantaneously: any related tension in the office dissipates, and everyone sighs with relief and gets back to work. No point in prolonging a painful situation.

Ultimately, no matter how careful you are when interviewing candidates, you are going to make mistakes. What's important is letting them go quickly before too much damage is done, before they bottleneck other team members' work or poison your culture. Besides, anyone I've let go has emailed me later, explaining that it was for the best. An employee might not be performing simply because it isn't a good fit, and letting them go provides them the freedom to open up their next door. That was certainly the case for me when I was let go from Abbott. Being laid off was a blow, even if it was not for anything I necessarily did wrong, but ultimately it set me on a more significant path sooner than I had expected. Be confident when you're firing someone, make sure that you listen to the person's concerns, answer their questions, and do so as soon as possible. Always treat everyone with dignity and respect.

In September 2015, months after our first attempt at using our product, we were still iterating to get it right. We had hired another talented engineer, Christina Skieller, earlier that year, and with her help, continued to make progress at a rapid clip. We had also found some physical space to work out of, an incubator called the Fogarty Innovation. It was founded by Tom Fogarty, a pioneer in the medical device industry. Anula had introduced me to one of their board members, Dr. Fred St. Goar, a veteran of the medical device field who not only sat on nVision's board as an observer, but was one of our biggest supporters, introducing us to everyone in his network.

With all of our new resources and designs, we were ready to go to Mexico for another clinical trial. We had built the end of our catheter with a clear material this time, so we could visualize whether or not the balloon was unfurling correctly. In doing that, we must have made the end of the catheter a bit less stiff, and therefore the balloon had less support, and our access rates plummeted to 50 percent. One device after another failed to deploy. We were stunned. How could we have gotten worse results than we had seen in our previous study? We went home that Friday feeling defeated.

I arrived at the office on Monday morning ready to start brainstorming with the team about what went wrong and how we could fix it. Jesus, knowing we needed additional strength from somewhere, already had new prototypes ready. Over the weekend, he had watched the films of the procedures we recorded, not just once but multiple times, trying to figure out a solution. If we increased the strength of any material, we would have to increase the size of the catheter. The more material, the bigger the catheter, and the more difficult insertion would be.

Jesus had found a way to increase the wall thickness of the

sheath in a way that did not increase the overall profile or size of our device. He walked me through the new prototypes while we watched the film of the previous study. Dave and I were convinced that Jesus had solved the problem, and we prepared ourselves for another trip to Mexico the following week.

Finally, success. The new device worked in every case, regarding both access and cell collection—thanks to Jesus, our savior.

I included Jesus in all clinical trials, and he agreed to come, even though he was deathly scared of flying. Jesus always wore a pair of lucky red socks on these trips. If we stayed at a particular hotel more than twice, the staff would know him by name and fall in love with him. He would get upgraded to any room he wanted.

I started to wonder, how was it that, though all of his previous bosses saw him as highly talented and he did work above and beyond a technician, no one had put "engineer" in his title? I talked to Dave, who agreed that we should give Jesus a promotion and additional equity, which the board had to approve. It took some convincing, but they agreed.

Sometimes as a leader, not only do you have to buck conventional trends when it comes to identifying talented employees but also with how you entice and retain them. A question that entrepreneurs often ask me is "How much should a particular position get in equity, title, or salary?" Using conventional metrics when making these determinations is fine, but don't apply them rigidly. The key question in figuring out a compensation package is "How important is this person to the success of the company and, thus, what should I do to retain them?"

Retaining talented people isn't only done through titles,

promotions, and money. If you consider your team La Familia, then their family is an extension of yours and should be treated as such. Every decade of life brings different requirements when it comes to taking care of family. People in their late twenties or thirties often need room to start families or take care of children. People in their forties and fifties have aging siblings and parents to attend to. Being sensitive to the needs of people coming from different generations can be difficult — sometimes you don't know what you haven't experienced or may never experience — but it's important to be as empathetic as possible. After all, it isn't only about "Are they getting the work done?" Sometimes, it's okay to pick up a person's slack or allow the work to fall behind for a limited time. I once rented a house for Wendy in San Francisco to cut down on her commute when our work extended well into the long evening hours. In another instance, I flew Jesus to Mexico so he could spend time with his family after a loss. We're all human, and humans need to take care of one another.

Another key to retention is asking yourself not only what the person can do for the company, but what the company can do for them. For example, Wendy always wanted more experience running clinical trials. Dave wanted to have a better grasp on maintaining a portfolio of intellectual property. If someone is performing well in their key areas, allowing them to expand their skill set is a great way to keep them challenged and satisfied. This is especially important for startups that statistically have such a low chance of success. In the case the company folds for whatever reason, don't you want the people who have given you years of their lives to have something to show for it, to gain more experience, and to grow in their skills and their value?

Any employees who stayed with nVision for more than one year not only gained new skills and expertise to add to their résumés but also experienced a secure, fun working environment, and they were able to take care of and spend time with their families. My team and our commitment to one another was, by far, the most rewarding part of my experience. *La familia, mi familia.*

Oh, and Jesus? He now wears a Rolex that I gifted him after the company sold. His eldest son just finished his first year of college. The most important lesson I learned in building nVision is that the best companies, like the best of families, take care of one another.

Back at this critical point of developing the device, the next step ahead of us was to gain FDA clearance and then raise another, larger round of funding. The FDA had never given clearance to a device that collected cells from the fallopian tube, nor had it cleared any device that traversed the full length of the fallopian tube. Hey, how hard could it be?

6

Shit Happens

Keep Going Through
Life's Ups and Downs

F alling to the floor is a recurrent theme in this story, and here I was, in June 2016, on the cold tile floor of my Chicago hotel room, crying. With everything I had been through and all of the rejection I faced, I had yet to shed any tears in front of anyone. Yet, I was now bawling my eyes out to a professional investor—the one who had put the most money in our company.

Darshana patiently listened on the other end of the phone, talking me through the details of what was making me so upset. How could a Series B fundraise make me so emotional? Yes, the deal terms were terrible and came as a surprise, but something else seemed to be going on. In fact, I wasn't just stressed—it was hormones. I was pregnant, I just didn't know it yet.

Raj and I had begun discussing starting a family, and we

wanted a baby. But now? Right in the middle of one of the most critical deals of the company's life? We were about to close a hard-earned financing of $12 million, one that I didn't want to jeopardize. I couldn't believe that I was pregnant. (I mean this literally. I didn't believe the + on the first test so I ran down the three flights of stairs of our apartment building to return to Safeway and buy more tests to confirm it.)

Sometimes bad shit happens that's troubling and distracting, and sometimes good shit happens that's equally distracting but wonderful, like expecting a child. "Work-life balance" is a misnomer, implying they should be given equal weight, with a "balance" between the two. Instead, work is just a part of life. When trying to give equal attention to everything, you can miss prioritizing another thing that's important—you. It's easy to forget about your own health, both physical and mental, when trying to keep all of the balls in the air. If you've had to face down doubters your entire life, getting those balls into the air in the first place is even harder. What are you supposed to do now? Let them all fall to the ground so that you can sleep more or have a little time to yourself? The more you feel you have to prove, the more likely you are to make decisions that may seem impressive and ambitious in the moment but can be self-sabotaging in the long run. I learned the hard way and made a fair share of mistakes in this department.

If you're working on building something that satisfies a good indignation, you often will try to make it all work and push everything forward, like I did. But you have to be okay with the fact that most likely, something unplanned, something that commands your attention, is going to crop up somewhere. If you can be flexible and accept that there will be curve balls, you'll be better prepared to handle them—and potentially let certain things go. I know that can be a challenge for many industrious personalities, especially when surrounded by doubters, as the pressure to prove oneself is a fierce driver.

Before I became a mother, this life lesson had not become clear to me. My team and I were all on overdrive trying to figure out the most effective regulatory strategy for a medical device—the next step to bringing the product to market. The first place to look for a viable path to approval is the FDA's database. We searched for any device that was even remotely similar to ours that had been cleared by the FDA. It was quickly evident that no one had collected cells from the fallopian tube. Our search did, however, reveal two products that were somewhat related. One was a device that collected cells from the uterus to look for uterine cancer. The second was something called Essure, a controversial device that left a piece of metal at the start of the fallopian tube, intentionally blocking the tube to cause sterilization.

While one of these innovations was in the ballpark of what we were trying to achieve, and the other was in the vicinity of where we were trying to go in the body, neither collected cells from the fallopian tube. We would be the first. That meant it would be harder to get FDA clearance because we didn't have a single device to compare ours to in terms of safety and effectiveness. I knew that in order to receive FDA clearance, I would have to work with a regulatory consultant who understood women's health inside and out. Every approval in the FDA database lists the name of the person who filed the request for approval. One name showed up again and again for women's health products: Cindy Domecus.

On LinkedIn, I learned more about her background and our common connections. I pondered who would provide the strongest introduction and asked them to send my information to Cindy. It worked (kind of). Cindy responded to my contact saying that she was in the middle of writing an application to the FDA and that she couldn't speak for at least three weeks. Even once we were introduced through email, she didn't respond for a week. I called her cell phone out of the blue and finally got her attention. Though I didn't realize it at the time, Cindy was so good and in such demand that companies would have to make their case before she would take them on as a client. Cindy has been a part of many successful women's health medical devices since the mid-1990s—everything from surgical robots that perform hysterectomies to life-saving devices that stop uncontrolled bleeding after childbirth.

The first time we spoke, she came across as professional and serious, and as if she didn't have a minute to waste, which she didn't. Not only did she have a lot of clients, she kept to her schedule. She has three children, and she arranged her schedule so that she could be there to greet and spend time with them every day when they got home from school. Fitting work into her life was important to her, and she was good at that balance. After thinking about it, Cindy decided that we were solving a real clinical need and she agreed to take us on as a client. Her demeanor held true once she started working with us—to say she is efficient is an understatement. It might be hard to get Cindy's time, but once you're on her calendar, what she can accomplish in one hour is astonishing. She's my favorite type of executive for early-stage companies, someone with years of experience but unafraid of doing the work herself, instead of just delegating every task. She's an expert in her technical field, regulatory consulting, but is also an articulate communicator, an invaluable skill when you're trying to explain complex products to the FDA. And what we were doing was certainly complicated.

Now that we had found the two devices most similar to ours, and we had a regulatory pro to guide us, we could start thinking through how to write the application for clearance. Before we could do that, we had to make decisions about the device; specifically, we had to determine just how far into the fallopian tube to go. On average, the fallopian tube is 10 centimeters, or about 4 inches, long. All evidence showed that the site of cancer was typically located at the very end of the fallopian tube, a full 10 centimeters away from the start of the fallopian tube, where it is embedded within the uterus. At the same time, cancerous cells could sometimes be found as far down as the uterus, or even the cervix, demonstrating that cells in the fallopian tube are constantly migrating. Therefore, we decided that it would be better to enter only the first 2.5 centimeters of the tube, which would make the procedure safer than going deeper. Additionally, the blockage-causing device I mentioned earlier, Essure, was also placed at about 2.5 centimeters. The FDA hadn't granted approval to a device to traverse the full length of the fallopian tube, but it had granted approval to a device that entered just the beginning portion of it, increasing their knowledge of that part of the anatomy.

We knew that the FDA had also cleared the device to collect

cells from the uterus. Since we were entering only the first 2.5 centimeters of the fallopian tube, which is contiguous with the uterus, we could argue that we were similar to the device that already received clearance. And our device was much less risky. Because the uterus is muscular and surrounded by blood vessels, perforating it with a catheter is more dangerous than poking a hole through the fallopian tube. Cindy decided that we could write an application for clearance, called a 510(k), citing the similarity to the device used in the uterus. Given how much she cares about the safety of anything introduced into the world of women's health, she asked us to collect some clinical data as well.

We went back to Dr. Garza, and together we would conduct a clinical study with ten subjects, or twenty fallopian tubes, and submit the resulting data to the FDA. Jesus built every device that we needed for this critical study and scheduled the procedure dates with Dr. Garza. We picked up vials of cytopreservative, the fluid used for preserving and transporting cell samples, from Dr. Pramanik, and we were on our way.

The study happened over several days, which gave the team a chance to spend time together in the evenings. The situation in Monterrey had stabilized by this point and we were able to sample amazing restaurants, including our favorite, La Nacional, which offered a modern take on traditional Mexican dishes. We had kept our previous trips as short as possible, so we'd never had time for such indulgences. One night, after an excellent meal and a few exceptionally good tequila flights, I returned to my room to find a complete disaster. The samples we had collected earlier that day, our precious samples, were leaking all over the bag they were stored in. This could have meant that even if we had been fortunate enough to collect cells, they could be lost. And the re-sults of the trial would show that we weren't able to collect cells even if we actually had. Luckily, if there was any contamination of the sample, we would see it under a microscope later.

I immediately called Jesus, Al, and Dave. One by one they arrived at my hotel room. All of us except Al had had a couple of drinks at dinner, but nevertheless, the team jumped into action. We needed something special to stop the leaking and make sure that whatever cells remained stayed inside of the vial. Putting our engineering minds together, boom! We had an epiphany: Saran Wrap.

Luckily, there was a convenience store across the street. I dashed off to buy a roll before it closed. Then we made an as-sembly line on the two full-size mattresses of the hotel room, methodically removing the caps from the sample vials, carefully applying the plastic wrap to the tops, and then replacing the lids. It worked; there was no more leaking. But would it hold? If they didn't have enough cells, we would still share the data with the FDA, but it could mean that the agency might blame the device and not the leaky vials. Alternatively, we could start the study over and write a report about what happened.

There was no crystal ball, no right or wrong answer, so I went with my gut. We submitted the samples. The results came back three days later—plenty of cells in good condition. It had been hard to listen to my gut and not my fear, but I am glad I did. When you are doubted by others, you end up doubting yourself as well. Finding that inner voice telling you what your gut wants to do, and listening to it, can be difficult. When shit happens, you have to make the hard calls and be willing to accept the consequences.

Remember: the worst possible thing to do is to not do anything at all. Make a decision and follow through on it.

After achieving strong clinical results, we sat down to write our 510(k). Cindy took the lead on outlining the document's big-picture strategy, and team members were assigned various portions to write. Our hours became even more grueling. After months of work, we submitted the file to the FDA. Then, we lost a week of review time because I forgot to pay the fee. My team had stayed at the office late, night after night, to get the file in as soon as possible, and just like that, my error had cost us a full seven days. I felt terrible, but that didn't help anything. Rather than beat yourself up when these things happen, learn from the moment, and then be gentle on yourself—accept that you make mistakes and forgive yourself. If you're going to feel any guilt, feel just enough to motivate you to put a process in place so the same mistake doesn't happen again.

Over the next six weeks, we went back and forth with the FDA, answering their numerous and detailed questions. They also requested that we conduct a clinical trial with the same design but with thirty to forty more subjects. Since we had already completed trying the device on ten patients, this would bring us to forty or fifty patients total. I decided to go the extra mile and chose forty patients. Al warned against this—why push our luck? I remained steadfast: I wanted to demonstrate to the FDA that we were thorough.

The new trial meant spending more weeks in Mexico, taking overnight flights and going directly into the operating room, followed by nights studying notes from the day's work or bonding over tequila. We had completed the study with thirty more patients, all of which were successful. Al again asked me if I wanted to go forward with ten more, and I said that I did. Plus, it had been written into the protocol that we would collect samples from forty people.

When it was time for our thirty-first patient, I noticed Dr. Garza suddenly pause in the middle of his procedure. Our balloon had managed to tear through this patient's fallopian tube. She was asleep under general anesthesia, and fortunately, she didn't feel any pain. This patient, like all of the patients in the trial, was about to have this entire part of her anatomy removed for other clinical reasons, but it was still shocking. Why would we perforate the fallopian tube now when we hadn't in thirty patients before? It was scary.

Dr. Garza kept his cool. After the procedure, he showed us images of the patient's fallopian tube, which was badly infected and therefore weak. He had injected dye into it, but found the dye wouldn't pass through because the tube was blocked. The combination of the blockage and the infection led to the perforation. Because of the blockage, the balloon had nowhere to go, so it exited through the fragile, infected wall. He said that this was to be expected under such circumstances and even that it probably would happen again if we encountered such a diseased fallopian tube. (But if a fallopian tube is that diseased, it wouldn't function anyway.)

As we continued the study over the next several weeks, we did not encounter another perforation. We submitted the new data to the FDA, disclosing everything that happened, and on

November 13, 2015, we received our first FDA clearance "to obtain cells from the proximal fallopian tube for cytological evaluation." We had work to do before we felt comfortable saying that we could diagnose cancer, and the FDA was far from allowing us to do that, but this accomplishment represented a great start toward that goal.

At the same time, I talked to several physicians about what our next studies might look like. I received the same feedback multiple times: we couldn't access only the proximal fallopian tube; we would have to go the full length. There was too great a risk that the cancerous cells wouldn't travel from the distal end to the fallopian tube, the site of origin of the cancer, to the proximal end—so we would miss cancers altogether. The team went back to the clean room to build devices. We also prepared to go down to Mexico for another study. The study itself would be designed the same way, but this time Dr. Garza would use a device that went the full length of the fallopian tube.

While the team was focused on our regulatory path, I focused on fundraising. This time, I would be seeking $12 million as part of my Series B for post-approval clinical studies. We had demonstrated that we could pick up healthy cells, but we had not yet demonstrated that we could capture malignant ones. The next study would be done in patients who were suspected to have ovarian cancer. Directly before their definitive diagnostic surgery, the physician would use our device and collect cells. We could then compare our results against the gold standard: fallopian tube tissue that had been cross-sectioned for microscopic examination.

If I was going to raise a Series B round of funding, I would have to start formulating a plan about how to commercialize the product once we had the necessary FDA clearances and reimbursement structure in place. To do this, I needed to beef up the business side of the team. I met Mika Nishimura, who had gone to Yale and Harvard Business School, through Anula, who had met her at a conference. She was polished and hardworking, though I suspect she had faced plenty of doubters because of her Japanese accent. I wasn't about to doubt her, especially after her consulting work for us to determine market size and opportunity stood out. I asked Mika to leave her consulting business and join us full time.

We were now in the fundraising process, and yet again, it was brutal. I was glad to have Mika's help. I put fundraising decks together, and she quickly and diligently came back with comments, or redid the slides, adding better graphics. We still struggled. It was 2015, but women's health still wasn't sexy. Despite all of the clinical data we had collected and the FDA clearance, most investors still didn't want anything to do with us. There was one potential backer, though, who represented a well-known fund and showed keen interest in what we were doing.

We had met serendipitously. I had been invited to be on a panel at a conference in San Francisco sponsored by Women 2.0. Founded in 2006, this nonprofit organization focuses on gender inclusion in the tech and startup spaces and offers resources for founders and professionals to grow their companies and careers. I rarely accepted engagements that would take my time away from nVision, but I believed in the goal of creating a network of female entrepreneurs, so I decided to attend. The topic of the panel I would speak on was also relevant: innovations in health care. Right before leaving for the talk, I took a rushed shower, which resulted in an extremely bad hair day, with no amount of blow-drying able to fix how puffy it was. I also wore a dress, which took me out of my comfort zone. I generally prefer slacks and a collared shirt but felt self-imposed pressure to "dress up" for this event.

The other panelists were far more established. One of them was a woman who was right out of Harvard Business School but still managed to raise her own venture capital fund. On this day, she was dressed to perfection, wearing expensive shoes and carrying a shiny designer handbag. The other panelists included a gentleman who is a well-known health care investor, and Camille (Cami) Samuels, then between jobs, having just left a venture fund named Versant.

As we waited in a back room before being led onstage, I sat with Cami. With her high cheekbones and gorgeous eyes, she immediately catches the attention of any room. She has degrees from Duke and Harvard and an undeniable track record as a venture capitalist, with huge wins like Genomic Health under her belt.

As we were waiting, one of the event organizers, a young entrepreneur, approached Cami and started to talk about her startup idea. Cami listened and then asked why she wanted to be an entrepreneur, to which the woman replied, "Power." Cami gently explained that power wasn't the right reason to be an entrepreneur. I joined the conversation and gave the same advice that I give anyone who asks me about starting a business or innovation: the only reason that someone should become an entrepreneur is that you deeply believe in the potential impact of what you're creating and the people it will help. Nothing besides your good indignation will sustain and motivate you through the long, arduous journey. Being an entrepreneur is hard and just not worth it otherwise. The somewhat dejected but, I hope, enlightened would-be entrepreneur thanked us and slinked away.

Once we got onstage, the panel was a lot of fun and well received by our audience. Everyone was engaged. I felt good about my performance, too. Cami and I walked out of the hotel where the conference was and chatted while she waited for her cab. She asked if we could grab a drink sometime. I was flattered and told her I would reach out. I didn't, but a month later, imagine my surprise when I received the following email:

> Hi Surbhi—
>
> This is a much-delayed note to say what a pleasure it was meeting you at the Women 2.0 conference. Your poise, insight, and calm—at such a young age—were really inspiring. Please let me know if I can be helpful to you in any way.
>
> Warmly,
> Cami Samuels

This was the first time that a well-known potential investor proactively reached out to me to connect. I was accustomed to being on the pursuing end when it came to high-caliber contacts. Cami was the first one to see something in me right away.

A week or so later, we met at a local wine bar. She opened up about her life; she had not had it easy. She had gone through two brutal divorces and was raising three boys, one with special needs, essentially on her own. I followed her lead, sharing details I wouldn't normally divulge in a first meeting, especially a business one. We discussed the challenges of being a professional woman, including balancing family life and dealing with sexism at work. We were both having fun, and we were both being ourselves.

A couple of months after this meeting, Cami emailed letting me know that she had joined Venrock, one of the most well-respected venture funds in Silicon Valley. I immediately congratulated her and included a brief update on my company.

A few months later, we met again for drinks. Of course, the dynamic was a little different now. I was aware that she was in a position to invest in my company. But the meeting was as relaxed and natural as the first one, and I think we both thoroughly enjoyed our heart-to-heart conversation. I wasn't fundraising quite yet, so I felt like the meeting was a friendly catch-up, with some professional chitchat thrown in.

Not until January 2016 was I ready to start speaking to investors about my Series B round. Cami expressed interest in making an investment in nVision. She spent an enormous amount of time working with me on my slide deck. We once met at the Battery in San Francisco, an exclusive club where she is a member, and she tore my deck apart and put it back together to create a much more compelling story.

As she did due diligence, she asked me all the right questions and was thorough, speaking with physicians to make sure my idea was a good one. Cami also pushed me to dream big. She was the person who convinced me that someone like the extremely accomplished Andrew Cleeland, a serial founder who had already sold two companies, could one day sit on my board. She told me how to deal with strategics, or larger companies, that might acquire my startup.

Finally, after several weeks of working together, she felt she had prepared me enough and that I was ready to pitch to her partnership. My team and I arrived at Venrock's beautiful office in Palo Alto, where the front desk attendant guided us to an equally striking conference room. My palms immediately started to sweat. I have rarely been that nervous in a pitch meeting and I was typically a good presenter, especially at this stage in nVision's history, because I was confident about my knowledge of the subject matter. But I absolutely bombed the partner meeting! Several years earlier, in 2013, I had pitched Venrock, pre-Cami. One of the partners had tripped me up. Unfortunately—and maybe I am just making excuses for myself—I carried that insecurity all the way into 2016.

I allowed the investors to control the meeting, a big no-no, going into the weeds of their questions instead of redirecting them to the most important parts of my message. Insecurity also drove me to invite my entire executive team to the meeting. I thought bringing an older, more experienced entourage to the table would help the Venrock team members take me seriously. All it did was put my insecurity on full display. Founders should feel confident in fundraising by themselves, and only bring other team members if they are requested by the investor. As I walked out of Venrock's office, I felt like I had lost one of the greatest opportunities put in front of me since starting nVision.

Cami called me soon after the meeting to deliver the bad news. As I suspected, the fund would not be investing. I apologized for not performing well. I felt like I had let her, and my entire team, down. I spent the rest of the day in bed.

Looking back, I wish I had been able to more quickly realize how much Cami believed in me. I wish that her belief in me would have prevented me from being so intimidated by her partners. I wish that her belief in me had translated to belief in myself. Sometimes, when you're underrated, you have to proactively fight off insecurity and focus on your strengths. If someone sees something in you, let them see it. Embrace it. Try to absorb it and see yourself from their standpoint. Don't assume they admire you because they don't know what they're doing—the feeling encapsulated in the old Groucho Marx line of not wanting to belong to any club who wants you as a member. They *do* know what they are doing, and that's why they think you have potential. You do want to be a member of that club.

I had learned my lesson about depending on only one investor to come through, and I was pursuing another investor simultaneously, but it was coming down to the wire. I had only a few more months left of payroll. Luckily, at this moment—if only for a moment—fundraising was going well. Karen Drexler, one of my early advisors, had introduced me to Jan Garfinkle, the founder of Arboretum Ventures, which invested in medical devices. We had a productive initial conversation on the phone, and as luck would have it, Jan, who was based in Ann Arbor, Michigan, was flying to San Francisco the next day. She asked if I could meet her for breakfast at the Rosewood, a hotel in Menlo Park known for the venture deals that get done there.

As I walked into the hotel restaurant (on time!), I looked around the large dining room and noticed dozens of other executives in the middle of their meetings. The location of the Rosewood on Sand Hill Road puts it in prime position for these sorts of professional get-togethers. Jan and I discovered we had so much to talk about. She also went to UC Berkeley, and after graduating had worked in the Bay Area as a leader at various medical device startups. When her husband accepted a job in Michigan, she went along. There wasn't much of a medical device investor scene there, but Jan is smart and industrious, and she decided to start her own venture fund. Today, only about 13 percent of venture capitalists are women. An even smaller number of funds are started by women. Jan managed to pull it off and build a reputation for successfully investing in health care startups.

As I went through my presentation, Jan asked many good questions, and when I was done, she told me she would get back to me once she got home. She didn't. I waited so I didn't appear desperate and I wrote to her a month later, in February. She responded by saying she was going on vacation. I didn't hear from her until March, but it had been worth the wait. She invited me to come out and meet the rest of the team. I flew to Ann Arbor from Mexico, after yet another trial. I snuck into a hotel near their office to freshen up before the meeting. The entire Arboretum Ventures partnership attended. I could tell that most of the partners weren't as interested in what I was pitching, but there was one person, Tom Shehab, who asked pointed, knowledgeable clinical questions and nodded appreciatively as I spoke.

Despite being 6 foot 5 inches and a former college football player, Tom had a gentle way about him. He went from being a practicing physician, to hospital leadership overseeing thousands of physicians, to then joining Arboretum as an investor. After the presentation, the investment team said they would get back to me shortly. I ran across the street to the famous Zingerman's Deli for a sandwich, which lived up to the hype.

As I was stuffing my face, standing next to my car in the parking lot, Tom appeared. He told me the presentation had gone well and that he would be in touch. Over the course of the next two months, he completed his investigation into the company alongside Jan. Our team met with them several times, as did our existing investors. The people at Arboretum were friendly and smart, and asked astute questions about pricing and how the product would be used. Their questions and recommendations even led us to revise some of our clinical trial plans. I was excited to have them as an investor and thought they would make a great addition to the board.

Finally, Arboretum sent us a term sheet detailing the conditions under which they would invest in the company. I was thrilled to receive it, but my excitement shattered when I read it. The firm wanted to own a huge percentage of the company. They asked for rights that would allow them to make unilateral decisions. At the time, I effectively controlled two board seats at nVision. They wanted to get rid of one of those two seats entirely, removing Anula (whom I had assigned to my second seat) from the board and assigning the other board seat to the "then-standing CEO" instead of the founder. All of this would put them in a better position to replace me as CEO if they ever wanted to. As my lawyer put it, they were reducing me from a founder to an employee. This is a terrible feeling for a founder; losing control of something that you built from the ground up feels like someone is trying to tear off one of your limbs. It's also rarely good for a startup to sideline a founder, the person who believes most in the product.

I thought about walking away from the deal. During one of those moments, I called Andrew Cleeland, to whom Dr. Fred St. Goar had enthusiastically introduced me, and he was willing to act as an informal advisor and help me think through the decision. I still couldn't believe I had his ear: Andrew was a legend in the medical device world. He had sold his first company for $1 billion and his second one for $500 million, in quick succession. He was adamant about my responsibility; he reminded me that my number one job was to keep the company alive—to do what was best for its future. I went back to Arboretum with two asks.

The first was to let Anula stay on the board, or to at least give me the option to choose who sits on the board for the seat she had. The second was to value the company higher, which would effectively give them less of a percentage ownership. They told me to choose one of the two; I could not have both.

I chose for them to give us a higher valuation and take less of the company. That turned out to be a mistake. They came up with a higher valuation but expanded the potential employee option pool, which effectively diluted the founders and previous investors even more than the original valuation they had offered. It's fine to allocate more equity to future employees, but the catch is that if the company is acquired and the option pool isn't assigned, it is split between the employees and the investors, thus increasing the new investor's yield. When I tried to negotiate further, they said take it or leave it. I was traveling so I asked for an extra day to get back home and discuss it with Rajeev. They wouldn't allow it.

That's when I found myself on that cold tile floor in Chicago calling Darshana to explain our newest predicament and bursting into tears, seemingly from the stress of it all, not yet aware of everything else that was going on in my body. Ultimately, I accepted the deal from Arboretum. I had no other choice. I had to give up control of the company so it could live. Though they had me sign the term sheet on May 20, they said they wouldn't be able to close the deal until July. They wanted to make sure we earned FDA approval for our device before giving us a dime. They were hedging their bets.

It was on June 1, one month before the money from Arboretum was to be wired, that I found out that another arrival was imminent. That's the day I took the two pregnancy tests and discovered I was expecting. A part of me wanted to wait until Rajeev got home, to make unveiling the surprise a romantic moment. But I couldn't wait, I was too anxious. I called Rajeev and said, "Babe, I'm pregnant." Stunned silence followed.

Once Rajeev and I got over our initial shock and allowed ourselves to get excited, I wanted to share it with my executive team as quickly as possible. I asked Wendy, Dave, and Mika to take a walk with me. We roamed until we reached a park near our office and took a seat on a bench. I was nervous—how would they take it? Would they think of me as irresponsible, needing to take time off work in our most demanding moments? Prioritizing my desire to start a family over building this company? Instead, they seemed overjoyed. When we finally finished our hugs, we sat back down and I shared with them my fears. Would I really be able to handle everything we had going on at work while tending to a new baby? They were parents themselves, so they offered advice from their experience. Wendy also told me about a podcast she had heard, about how parents become more productive at work because they don't feel like they have a minute to spare. Then, each one of them reassured me by telling me that they were happy to take on more responsibility and step up to the plate whenever needed.

If you're going to have any shot at the mythical work-life balance, then team members who are empathetic and willing to step into things outside their usual area of focus are required. They are ready to wear any hat necessary to get the job done. And they understand that there will be a time when they need someone to step up to the plate for them and carry more of the load; they aren't worried about the workload being equal at all times. You want to hire the type of people who like to be there for one another. At the same time, leaders of companies and startups should try to ensure that there are enough people in their workplace so that employees don't feel overloaded (while making sure there is an adequate amount of work for everyone to do, or they might see their culture suffer).

Next, I had to decide whether to tell Arboretum that I was expecting. Anula and Darshana, who were delighted and supportive, both advised that Arboretum didn't need to know yet. I grabbed lunch with Andrew and revealed the situation. "First of all," he said, "this is good news. Why are you stressed out about this? This is the most beautiful thing that could happen to you." He also agreed that I shouldn't feel any pressure to tell Arboretum. After all, I was so early on in my pregnancy that I didn't even tell most of my friends about it.

I now know that my advisors were correct. Sharing personal

information with employees and others associated with your company can be a bonding experience, but it's also okay if there are lines that you don't want to cross. It's okay to think about how people might react to your news. If you're not interested in sharing something personal, don't—just remember the trade-off that coworkers can't help support you if they don't know what's going on. Whether or not you're ready to share it, carrying a child, or wanting to spend time with one, is a beautiful thing. Life happens, and this is the best example of it. I wish I had truly believed this at the time, instead of agonizing about the decision and being fearful someone might "suspect" I was pregnant. When Tom came to town and asked me to go to dinner, I ordered half a glass of wine because I didn't want him to think anything suspicious was going on. That's how far I let the situation go.

The round of money was sent on July 12, 2016. I had signed the term sheet with only a couple of months of money left in the bank, and had the wire from Arboretum come even two days later, I wouldn't have been able to complete nVision's next payroll cycle using company funds. Raj and I tried to figure out if we had enough to pay my employees using our personal bank account. Needless to say, this financial uncertainty placed a great deal of stress on me and my pregnancy.

After the money was wired, Arboretum became a great partner. Negotiations can be tough. After all, they were doing their job in trying to extract the most from the deal with nVision while also reducing their own risk. It's sort of like planning a wedding with your in-laws. Terrible when you're in it, but they can turn out to be excellent grandparents. Plus, Arboretum were the ones who believed in me and who were ready to put funds on the table when no one else was. Though we routinely engaged in a healthy debate about the direction of the company, Arboretum and nVision worked together well after I accepted their money. I did of course eventually tell them about my pregnancy, and they were supportive.

Arboretum and I decided we wanted to bring an independent member onto the board, someone who was neither a founder nor an investor. My mind immediately went to Andrew; he had already helped so much without asking for a formal agreement. I recalled our first meeting, when he agreed to meet me for breakfast at the Rosewood. Instead of focusing on operational issues the company was facing, we ended up talking about our teams because of how important they are to us. And we both cried. Andrew told me a story about how he had created an environment so supportive at his startup that someone, for the first time in their professional career, came out of the closet and discussed being gay. He was proud of that, and humbled by it. We connected and I never forgot that conversation. When thinking about who should be an independent board member, I always wanted it to be Andrew. I was honored that even though he could choose to sit on the boards of numerous companies, he chose to sit on mine.

It had been a tough battle to get the money. I'd had to give up a lot of ownership of the company as well as control over it, but now we had what we needed to continue making progress and running even harder clinical trials. We decided that the team should leave Fogarty Innovation, the incubator that we had been in the last couple of years. We needed a new space that would accommodate our growing company. Once I found the right office, Mika took it from there and did everything from negotiating an extensive contract to hiring movers while I was very pregnant.

With the new money that we raised, we conducted our clinical study in patients who were suspected to have ovarian cancer. Right after we collected a cell sample, these women had their fallopian tubes and ovaries removed, which was already part of their treatment plan. Their fallopian tubes would be dissected and examined under a microscope for cancer as part of the standard pathology work-up. We would compare the results of the cell samples we collected with those pathology results, which is the gold standard for detecting cancer.

We completed the study ahead of schedule and obtained results earlier than expected. The results were groundbreaking. Out of the five times that the gold standard detected malignancy in the fallopian tube and we were able to retrieve a sample (the anatomy of those patients was harder to navigate given the progression of their disease), our device also found that there were malignant cells. It was a small amount of data, to be sure, but it was promising. We had more than half the money we needed in the bank, and I felt good about starting a larger study and trying to replicate our findings on a bigger scale. Not only that, larger companies heard about our results through their physician networks and wanted to learn more. Maybe in this phase, hiring—and, when we eventually needed more money, fundraising—would finally be easier.

But, again, life happens. This was around the time I woke up in a puddle, my bedsheets soaked through. I thought maybe

I peed myself? My water wasn't broken, it couldn't possibly be broken. My due date was a full eight weeks away, two months. It was 6:00 a.m., and I woke up Rajeev. He told me to go back to sleep, our meetings didn't start until 9:00 a.m. that day. I tried to explain the situation as calmly as I could, trying not to betray my panic. He knows me well, though, and he shot out of bed. Fear crept into his expression. *Please let this be pee*, I thought to myself. I stuck my nose near the stain and took a deep whiff of the large peanut-shaped marking on the bed. There was no smell. It wasn't pee, it was amniotic fluid.

I called my gynecologist. She said, "Get here as quickly and as safely as you can. You won't be leaving the hospital without a baby in your arms." She said this not to scare me but to prepare me mentally for what was about to happen. Rajeev grabbed a bag of clothes and toiletries, and brought the car as close to our apartment as possible. I waddled to the passenger seat and sat on a pile of towels, wishing that they would somehow stop the loss of fluid. We zoomed over to the hospital and got there just in time. As they took me out of a wheelchair and onto a bed, the contractions started. What I remember next is a flurry of forms. The hospital staff said they wanted to give me a shot to stop my contractions and that it would feel like I drank ten cups of coffee. But they needed to hurry and get the approval; the contractions were getting stronger and stronger.

The injection was worse than they described. My heart felt like it was uncontrollably beating out of my chest. My sister and mom dropped everything and made it to the hospital. They tried to comfort me as I writhed in pain and fear. Everything hurt. Raj held my hand. Would our baby be okay? There is a big difference between being pregnant and being a mom—this was the jarring start of my transition.

The medication did its job and my contractions came under control. The medical staff ran a battery of tests and told me that they didn't understand why my water broke, but that they thought I was producing enough amniotic fluid to stay pregnant for a bit longer. At that point, I was thirty-two weeks pregnant, and they said if I could make it to thirty-four weeks, the baby would have a much better chance at a full recovery. The extra two weeks would allow the doctors time to give me shots that would accelerate the baby's lung development. Still, they said, there was a 95 percent chance or higher that they would need to assist him with his breathing when he was born.

During the two weeks I was on bed rest in the hospital, we lost the baby's heartbeat a total of seven times. Seven times I was carted to the operating room for an emergency C-section, but the baby's heartbeat would miraculously reappear right before the procedure. Rajeev slept on a cot, which was more like a rock, right next to me, never leaving my side even for a night. My mom and sister arrived every day with my favorite meals. One of my closest friends, Julia, showed up at the hospital daily during my stay, while her husband, Max, played handyman at our house, getting it ready for our arrival. Opal, my friend from high school, flew in from Cincinnati to see me, right in the middle of her residency. She stayed on through the birth. More friends piled on. Chrissy designed the baby's nursery, Kim set up our stroller and everything else that needed to be ready by the time we got home. Aruna helped us decide on a name by drawing cartoons of what she pictured for the different names we selected. Shawn made us laugh. My team checked in with me regularly, and it seemed like everything was moving along. My tribe showed up and got me through those difficult weeks.

Even while in the hospital, I didn't stop working. I had a board meeting scheduled, and I refused to cancel it. I even made my executive team join me at my bedside, though I was in a gown. Andrew called me before the meeting and told me that it was foolish to go ahead and that he was asking me not only as a friend but with the authority of a board member to cancel it. I refused. Arboretum had just invested in me, and I felt I had something to prove. We were in such a good place as a company, and I was afraid they would think less of me. I took the meeting, asking the other board members to ignore the beeping of the monitors and the chattering of nurses in the background. In case it wasn't obvious, I should have listened to Andrew. At that point, I should have started taking care of my body and focused on my family, instead of continuing to expose myself to stressful situations. Life was happening, work could have waited.

I made it to thirty-four weeks, and Shreyas Sarna Behera was born by C-section on December 18, 2016, weighing 4.5 pounds. I got to hold him briefly, his small body on top of my chest, before they whisked him away to the NICU. The nurse, I am sure in an effort to motivate me to get moving, told me that I could see him in the NICU as soon as I was able to take a few steps.

A few hours after my C-section, I managed to get myself to the NICU. I put my hand against the glass of the incubator and peered at my newborn son. Some people say that falling in love with your child takes a while, which I understand. But I had spent the last several weeks constantly agonizing over whether he was going to be okay, so for me it was love at first sight.

The machine kept him warm, a necessity because he couldn't maintain his own body temperature. A chorus of monitors beeped both reassuringly and hauntingly. My water had broken eight weeks early, and we had almost lost him. Now, looking at his tiny body, I wondered when I would be able to take him home, to keep him warm using my own skin instead. Even though I knew it was scientifically inaccurate to blame myself, I couldn't stop the infamous mother's guilt from seeping into my thoughts: this was all my fault. The professional choices that had confronted me over the past two years had been numerous and difficult. And they had, in some ways, brought me to this point—sitting in a wheelchair, my head resting against the side of the incubator, thinking about all the things I would have done differently.

There is plenty of confusing data out there on the cause of preterm birth. One study demonstrated that premature births dropped by up to 90 percent during the pandemic, though they don't know exactly why—it could have been due to reduced physical activity or stress for women in lockdown, or because the air quality improved with fewer cars on the road. The doctors kept telling me that my stress levels had nothing to do with my baby coming early. The nurses told me that his umbilical cord had been wrapped around his neck three times, and that my water breaking was nature's way of getting Shreyas out of a precarious situation. Still, I blamed myself. Looking back, I would have given up any amount of company success to prevent Shreyas's early birth. But I'm not sure that was a trade-off I would have had to make, anyway. Even if we delayed timelines so I could concentrate on my health, we would done well—maybe better—after all, we were building something people needed. Now, Shreyas is healthy and thriving.

Back then, my guilt didn't stop me from working after he arrived. Shreyas was born on the eighteenth, I announced the birth to my team on the nineteenth, and joined meetings on the twentieth. Though the meetings were on the phone and not in person, I still felt so torn about it. But instead of figuring out some sort of balance, or contemplating other solutions, I just plowed ahead with everything, my fear of the company failing dominating all other concerns one minute, my fear of not spending enough time with my baby dominating the next. Wasn't my health worth risking if it meant that I could improve women's health as a whole? As much as the bundle in my arms created a new dimension of myself, as much as I loved him, I couldn't stop now.

Even then, part of me knew that I would need to learn how to change what I prioritized. Pushing my boundaries is one thing; pushing them off a cliff is another. When you're building a company or driving a project toward a certain goal, you can become blind to everything else. Especially if you're underrated, you can be relentless—and that can get in the way of your own well-being. And you cannot be successful if you are not well. Your health matters.

Life happens. Shit happens. Depend on your tribe. Don't think you need to be everywhere at the same time. Slow deadlines down, move things around. This is not only good for you and your family but also for whatever goal you are working toward. If you aren't able to sustain your health and happiness, you and your business are bound to falter, and might even fail. I know how hard it is to allow yourself to do that, that it's easier said than done, but try it.

We were able to leave the NICU nine days after Shreyas was born, on December 27. Soon after, I received an email from Boston Scientific. They had learned that we had gathered valuable data from our clinical trial. Could they know more? Their business development team would be in town on January 9, and could I meet with them at the Marriott Marquis downtown? This would be just three weeks after I gave birth through a major abdominal surgery, with a premature baby at home. What do you think I did?

7

Letting Go

Knowing When to Make a Change

Just ten days after leaving the hospital with our son, I sat in the lobby of the Marriott Marquis, waiting for Boston Scientific's representatives to arrive. Today was a big meeting, one where we would talk about ways our companies could work together, and I felt like I couldn't afford to miss it. I think, however, that they were surprised to see me!

I had met with Boston Scientific, and specifically Colin Morrison, part of the women's health business development group, several times before. Two years earlier, he visited the office, and we spent hours discussing nVision. We grabbed lunch at my favorite Indian restaurant, Amber, and over butter chicken, I detailed everything from our intellectual property strategy to marketing plan.

Now I had even more substantial updates to share. By this point, we had early data demonstrating that we could pick up cancerous cells from the fallopian tube. We also didn't have any false positives, meaning that we hadn't mistakenly stated that malignant cells were present when in fact they weren't. The meeting went well, and Colin seemed genuinely interested in partnering with us in some way. We talked about what devices were in their portfolio and possibly collaborating on a clinical trial. The company was also interested in the possibility of investing in us the next time we were raising a round of capital. I hadn't considered the possibility that Boston Scientific might want to acquire us, and Colin didn't bring it up. Though I was glad I summoned the energy to attend the meeting, by the time I got home, I was absolutely exhausted, even though it was just an hour long. I was still healing from my C-section, and with a newborn at home, I was sleep deprived.

But there was little time to catch up. About a week after the meeting with Boston Scientific, four weeks after I gave birth, Wendy called. She was calm but had alarming news. Even if the team could somehow keep the work afloat, they disagreed about everything from product improvements to regulatory strategy. I had not left clear directions in terms of who would make decisions. I had assumed that the head of each function would make decisions when it impacted their group. But this was shortsighted. What happens if there are cross-functional decisions (decisions between different groups at the company) that need to be made? A few months before, I had realized this could be a potential issue and was in the process of exchanging emails with the board about a possible plan when my water broke early. But we ran out of time and resolving this fell through the cracks. Now the company was struggling.

Wendy knew that what she was asking was a big deal, but she requested that I come back into the office, ending my "maternity leave." Though I had never stopped working—including answering emails and taking calls on the day I gave birth—I hadn't been to the office. I was torn on whether I was supposed to be at home or at work, but I also felt that I couldn't let her or the company down. So, the very next day, I went in. I wanted to keep the company alive, I wanted it to thrive, even if it meant doing things that might be to my own detriment.

With the delineation of tasks and responsibilities unclear while I was out, frustrations mounted and tensions boiled over between the team. I tried to remedy the friction by holding meetings between functional groups and hearing their concerns. I encouraged discussion, but for situations that had been lagging, I made quick decisions so that no one felt blocked. With the prior decision-making flow and process back in place, within a week or so, things normalized. Though I again heard laughter in our halls, I wish I had simply assigned someone full decision-making authority before I left, instead of worrying how others might react to my choice. A lot of what happened could have been avoided. But at least the mistake wasn't fatal.

As happy as I was about this turnaround, I was waking up several times a night, every hour and a half or so, to check on or feed my premature baby. *Is he still breathing? Still staying warm?* I was constantly worried about him and constantly anxious about the company. If I was with the baby, I felt guilty about not being with my employees. If I was with employees, I felt guilty about not being with the baby. I didn't realize I was in a constant lack-of-sleep and guilt-induced state of anxiety. During this time, Rajeev mentioned that I was often unable to finish sentences and would trail off without making my point, staring into space.

Still, I couldn't let my foot off the gas even if I had very little gas left in the tank. This was nVision's busiest period yet. We were continually enrolling patients in our study. Clinical studies are a massive effort that take place across multiple states and for which most companies engage a clinical research organization (CRO) to help with the workload. Instead, we were doing every part of it ourselves—from finding the sites and getting contracts signed to attending the actual cases. We decided that we would keep the quality of the study as high as possible, instead of contracting out this most important work. I had heard horror stories of CROs derailing studies of other companies and didn't want to take the risk. Dr. Bethan Powell, a practicing gynecologic oncologist from Kaiser Permanente San Francisco, our principal investigator of the study, would sometimes call us with twenty-four-hour notice—you can't always plan when a cancer patient needs surgery—and we would have to drop everything and attend. At the same time, we were going to the FDA for yet another clearance. To intensify matters further, it turned out there were many companies interested in investing in or partnering with us. I was tasked with attending more meetings and providing endless amounts of information to fulfill their requests. In the spring, about six months after I gave birth, the American College of Obstetricians and Gynecologists (ACOG) held its annual meeting. It attracts thousands of gynecologists from around the world, as well as numerous companies involved with women's health. Because there wasn't a huge amount of innovation in women's health, many of the larger medical device companies that had divisions for women's health had heard of us, often through common clinical advisors. As a result, four large companies were interested in meeting with us during the conference to learn more about nVision. It was never made totally clear why they wanted to meet, and it was hard to ask them why without sounding desperate. Was it to get to know smaller companies in the space for a potential collaboration around a clinical study? Or an investment? Maybe even an acquisition? Whatever it was, I was surprised they wanted to get together for any reason at all. It's a confusing transition to go from being doubted to desired, but again, when people show interest, you have to take the interest at face value and embrace it. I knew I was going to find out what the larger companies wanted soon enough.

I was aware I had to muster up the energy to engage in discussion with these larger companies. Finding funding for medical devices in general is difficult, and especially so for my industry. I couldn't let the opportunity to impress them pass me by. But how would I find the time? The bandwidth?

At that point, my mom, Anu, came to my rescue. My mom had been coming to the house almost daily to take care of Shreyas and, frankly, to take care of me. Though I was breast-feeding, I would be busy from the moment I woke up, and would routinely forget to eat breakfast, and then push lunch to 2:00 p.m. It was my mom who constantly tried to remind me to pay attention to my health and who would show up to my desk with a balanced meal.

This couldn't have been an easy time for her either. My mom

was entangled in a divorce from my dad that she had initiated about five years earlier. It is hard to get divorced in your fifties (it's always hard to get divorced). She hadn't worked outside of the home, and her family had always been her primary focus, so she felt a great deal of displacement no longer carrying on the role of a spouse. Finally, though, she had found a rhythm on her own. She now had her own place in Fremont and a new set of recently divorced friends. They took turns going on walks with or cooking for one another, and Mom was loving traveling. She was also teaching Hindi on a schedule that worked for her. At last, I thought, my mom was happy.

Despite all of her success at creating a new independent life that she enjoyed, she offered to give so much up to move in with us. Raj was also running his own company, which had hundreds of employees, so we both readily agreed.

Having a premature baby can lead to many health problems, so Raj and I worried about everything, which included hiring someone to help at home, so watching Shreyas became my mom's full-time job. I wished there were specialists in premature baby care, but I couldn't find any, though these were not options we could afford anyway. My mother was a powerhouse. She didn't just watch the baby. She managed the entire household: planning meals, grocery shopping, organizing everything. While she released some of the guilt I felt about not being around Shreyas all of the time, I felt bad that she was giving up her new life. Some of that was alleviated by the bond I witnessed between my mom and her grandson. This wasn't something she was doing just for me, she was now back commanding a role she had always excelled at and enjoying it even more as a grandmother.

I was especially grateful and relieved to have the help at home because the meetings at ACOG went well. These larger companies that wanted to chat with me were considering buying nVision, and they were asking me questions about the business almost constantly. Their questioning ran much deeper than anything a venture capitalist had asked us in the past. Venture capitalists invest in a variety of companies, so it's hard for them to be experts in any one area. The people who were now researching nVision had worked on women's health every day for decades and knew the space even better than I did.

I was starting to thoroughly burn out. Exhausted, I didn't have the clarity to properly think through the existential questions I was facing. Did I really want the company to be acquired? We were doing well, had plenty of money in the bank, and our next steps were apparent to me. At the same time, I thought that maybe we could get the device to patients quicker if we had the resources of a big company. And that's what nVision was all about—the patients.

Andrew Cleeland, having sold companies in the past and now on the board as an independent director, knew that discussions with the larger companies were getting serious. Because several interested parties were at the table, he advised that we should engage an investment banker. An investment banker can either help companies in trouble try to sell before they implode, or they can help a successful company get the highest possible price when there is a group of interested buyers. When a company is in the process of being bought, as mine was, these bankers can be a helpful go-between to guide the process. Andrew knew one of the best in the business: Rakesh Mehta (Rak), who then worked at J.P. Morgan. Remembering that someone had told me "Rak doesn't get out of bed in the morning for less than two hundred million dollars," I expressed doubt to Andrew that Rakesh would give nVision the time of day.

Andrew recognized my worth and nVision's even if I didn't, so he called Rak in front of me while I sat in his office. Rak immediately agreed to a meeting later that same week. When the appointment came, he showed up almost thirty minutes late. Evidently, I had some serious competition in the late department. I kept glancing out my window, and there I saw Rak, pacing back and forth in our parking lot, phone to his ear, a serious look on his face.

He immediately broke the stereotypical image of an investment banker: male, tall, white, and arrogant. Rak was a man, but once he came into the office, I realized that he was none of the other things. He was confident, yes, which was evident by both his steady gaze and his self-possessed gait, but he's brown and doesn't give the impression of an aggressive finance dude. Not something you see often at his level. And when he was finally across the table from me, I could tell I had his attention.

He had clearly spent time on the materials I had sent in advance. At that point, I asked him point-blank why he would take on nVision as a client. He didn't blink. "I'm not going to shit you, it's because I know companies will want to buy what you have." Later I learned the reason he was late to our meeting had nothing to do with arrogance, or doubts about me or nVision. It was because he was in the middle of backing out of a billion-dollar deal—even though he would have made a ton of money—because he thought the acquiring company was shortchanging the smaller company.

For Rak, it wasn't all about the money. I once asked him what he did to celebrate a two-billion-dollar sale. He replied, "I bought myself another bike-riding vest." He talked about his Punjabi wife and his daughter with such affection and adoration. I like to think that Rak took me on not only because he thought he could sell the company but also because, without a doubt, he wanted to create more examples of successful brown women for his daughter.

While I had been focused on the deal-making, the team kept the company afloat operationally, and we were back to smooth sailing. Once again, Boston Scientific visited our office for a meeting. To my surprise, this time Colin brought about a dozen people with him, with a representative from every functional area. Imagine presenting a regulatory or reimbursement strategy to someone who only does that every day—and in the area of women's health. I made a joke about taking them to our "large conference room," a ten-by-twelve-foot box that could barely hold us all. We had to remove the artificial ficus trees from the corner just to squeeze everyone in.

Other companies were doing their due diligence on nVision but not going to the same depth as Boston Scientific. They knew where the greatest risks were and spent the most time looking at our clinical and insurance reimbursement strategy. They watched us assemble a device, making sure that the design was actually something scalable in manufacturing. Importantly, I noticed that our teams got along, with serious discussions founded on respect and punctuated by laughter.

Because the meeting spanned all day, I had to leave the group several times to pump breast milk; otherwise, I would feel uncomfortable. The third time I dismissed myself, I decided to tell the visiting team where I was going. I didn't want them to think I was taking cigarette breaks or guzzling from a flask in the restroom. Instead of reacting in an uncomfortable and stiffly formal way, one of the men encouraged me with a casual "Oh yeah, go do that! My wife feels so much better afterward." Colin had a glass of water waiting for me when I got back. At this point in the process, I knew that if the device was going to land with someone, if nVision was going to have a new home, I would want it to be Boston Scientific. Colin emailed me afterward, thanking me for the time and letting me know he thought the meeting went well.

And then . . . radio silence. I still wasn't getting much sleep. My schedule was packed with reciting the ins and outs of our business to potential acquirers. Every meeting I attended was more important than the last one. One company sent representatives to watch a clinical trial case—could anything be more nerve-racking? Another one asked me to fly across the country to meet their CEO, only to surprise me with a team of engineers instead. But the silence from my first-choice buyer was the worst.

While I was working on keeping up with external demand, Wendy was left making key internal decisions for the company. Right before I gave birth, we had hired two excellent team members to assist her. Katherine helped her with all things quality related, and Alan worked on manufacturing strategy. But they had been pulled away from that to support our clinical trial, which was incredibly demanding. I once emailed with the subject line "please stop working!" to Wendy and the entire executive team, because I could see that at 9:00 p.m. they were all working away on a shared document. Wendy responded at 11:00 p.m. saying that she was done with her tasks and apologizing for "not seeing" my earlier email.

Everyone on the team was working like Energizer Bunnies. They just kept going. Mika made a model of our market so robust that even when ten marketing representatives from an acquirer were hurling questions at us a mile a minute, no one could stump us. Even though she had a background in commercialization and marketing efforts, she was contributing a great deal to our clinical efforts by meeting with physicians and tracking all our clinical data. I could always count on Mika, for anything. Even with her pedigree, she came to the table with no ego at all, no task was too complex or too small.

But even with all-star teammates who went above and beyond, burnout seemed impossible to prevent. How was I going to choose between seeing nVision to the finish line and spending time with my son? I started doing crazy things to keep up. I would pump breast milk on my commute home from work, trying to make the experience as hands-free as possible with the right bra. In hindsight, probably not the safest thing—and a bit embarrassing whenever a large truck would pull up next to me at a red light, the driver clearly being able to see down into my car if they just turned their head. If I needed to travel, even to Europe, I did it in the shortest amount of time possible. I took overnight flights, went to the meeting, and headed right back to the airport. The baby guilt drove me to obsess over how much breast milk Shreyas was getting, despite the fact that formula is scientifically proven to be safe. If I was on the East Coast, I shipped my milk in special refrigerator packaging back to San Francisco.

One of the major milestones we had coming up was a meeting of our scientific advisory board (SAB). Most medical device and pharma companies have such boards, which consist of scientific and medical experts in the space. We had just enrolled our last patient in the study, demonstrating that we could collect cancerous cells from the fallopian tube and were ready to review the data with the board. There was a mix of gynecologists, oncologists, pathologists, and molecular scientists in the room. The board thought our data was compelling so far, but 44 patients and 5 cancer samples are small numbers. The experts were looking forward to the next study we would do, which would be more statistically significant with 150 patients. We would submit that study to the FDA, so alongside everything else underway, we started to plan that out as well.

We were lucky enough that Dr. Powell decided to do this study with us again. Though she was always professional, she was never overly friendly as she wanted to keep her distance and be as scientifically minded as possible. At the SAB meeting, we had sandwiches brought in for lunch. Dr. Powell refused to take one because she was worried about creating a potential conflict. *Was the sandwich a form of compensation?* She saw nVision as the company sponsor and wanted to remain completely independent. She played the devil's advocate (or the patient's advocate, as the case may be) with us, and that was one of the many reasons I appreciated working with her. To complete the study in a timely manner, we needed more clinical sites. Dr. Powell had another colleague join the study from a different Kaiser site in Oakland.

In addition, we had Dr. Charles Landen from the University of
Virginia as an investigator. Not only was he a gynecological oncologist, but he was also one of the pioneers behind the theory
that ovarian cancer actually begins in the fallopian tube.

We had built a hardworking, experienced team and were
making exponential progress, but we were all feeling crushed
under the weight of the tasks before us. We were wondering if
we really could pull it off. That's when I received an email from
one of our angel investors, a physician from the Cleveland Clinic.
Sadly, his cousin had just been diagnosed with advanced-stage
ovarian cancer. He wrote to me to remind me of the importance
of the work we were doing and how he wished his cousin had the
benefit of the nVision device. I forwarded it to the team. Wendy
responded with "Patients are waiting." As exhausted as we were,
we kept pushing on.

And I kept burning out. And so did my mom. And so did
Wendy. I tried to carve out time for my family. Every Friday, I
came home from the office around noon to be with Shreyas. But
I would end up getting distracted by email or a phone call, and
then try to multitask, which was incredibly frustrating because
I felt like I wasn't paying enough attention to work or the baby.
While the baby was happy to be bounced as I walked around the
house with him, or held up his rattle, I was missing out on the
moment by not being fully present.

In retrospect, there are many things I would have done differently during this time that could have prevented me from
burning out, and there are many tricks I implement today that
help tremendously. First, determine what a fulfilled life means
to you. For me, it's that I want to live in such a way that allows

me to be fully present in whatever moment I am in, instead of being worried about what is coming next or going on elsewhere. In addition to working on something meaningful, I want time for myself and my family, and the space to do what is important to me without feeling pressure to always be perfect at any of it. I want to grab dinner and a drink with a girlfriend every couple of weeks. And I want to be okay with that.

Once you've decided what you want out of life, determine what that means for what you can give to work and your other pursuits—and what has to give, because something does, and it can be hard to let go. Be deliberate about how you spend your time. Determine how much time you want to spend with your loved ones each day. Don't worry about scheduling it yet. Just think about the number of hours that will make you feel fulfilled with that aspect of your life. It could be two, three, four, eight hours. No right or wrong answer exists. Once you know how many hours, schedule them into your daily life. Put them on your calendar. You might readjust the time every Sunday evening when reviewing your schedule for the week, but at least start with an estimate of when you'll get those hours in. No one ever heard someone on their deathbed saying, "I spent too much time with family."

If you don't start with determining how many hours you want to spend with your family, work will slowly creep into absolutely everything. There is no limit to how much work you can do, or how much you feel should be done, if you're building your own ladder and have doubters around you. It is unending. So decide how much time you want to spend doing things besides work and make *that* a hard line.

Now, the next part is even more difficult. Once you've decided how much time you want to spend with your family, and you start to implement it, try not to feel guilty. Remind yourself of the complexities of the situation—and that you're doing your best given the circumstances. Guilt uses an enormous amount of emotional currency that is better spent in other ways. Be thoughtful when you come up with the number of hours you want to spend, and then make peace with it. Again, this isn't to say that you can't adjust, increasing or decreasing in a deliberate fashion, but don't second-guess yourself constantly.

This strategy will enable you to do one thing better: focus on what is front of you. If you're a type A multitasker like me, you may think the more tasks you're doing at the same time, the better. While it might seem impressive to show off your mad skills in this area, it's bad for you. It destroys your ability to be present, just like guilt does. If you're with your kid or doing something you enjoy, at least for a set period like twenty minutes, put your phone away. In her book *Thrive*, Arianna Huffington calls cell phones our binkies. I couldn't agree more. We don't need a binky—we do need to be present in the moment to truly live.

If you do the above and throw in some meditation—even ten minutes a day—not only will you feel better, but your work will be higher quality. Being present is not only better for you, but better for everyone and everything around you, including your work. American workers across the board saw heightened rates of burnout in 2021, according to the American Psychological Association's Work and Well-being Survey. A whopping 79 percent of people said they had experienced work-related stress in the month before the survey. Nearly 3 in 5 employees reported negative impacts of work-related stress, including lack of interest, motivation, or energy (26 percent) and lack of effort at work (19 percent). Meanwhile, 36 percent reported cognitive weariness, 32 percent reported emotional exhaustion, and 44 percent reported physical fatigue—a 38 percent increase since 2019. These numbers are staggering.

But here comes the *really* hard part. Lower. Your. Standards. I wouldn't hire a nanny because my mom, Rajeev, and I were worried about our premature baby being in the hands of someone unable to care for him the way we did. Wendy and I didn't want to use a CRO because we thought they wouldn't do as good of a job as we could. We would conduct interviews with people for various positions but never hire them, because we feared that they just weren't perfect enough. Our own impossible standards might have been part of our success—it's hard to say—but maybe if we had accepted help when we were drowning, we would have gotten the same results and kept our sanity.

This can apply to your personal life as well. Maybe your partner doesn't boil the spaghetti for the kids just as perfectly as they like it—for eight minutes and fifteen seconds—but if the kiddos are hungry, they'll eat it. We have to stop and think about whether this is the case when we feel overwhelmed but are also unwilling to bring in extra eyes, ears, and hands. Maybe no one will ever work as hard or care as much as an owner or founder, or a parent. But you can't succeed on your own without destroying yourself. Perfectionism gets in the way of progress and mental health. Lower your standards.

Especially if you're a woman, or a new mom, please remember

that you need to be on your own priority list. I sometimes bristle at books or advice blogs that tell you to sleep. I mean, as if that's even a choice for a new mom. Way to add pressure to do something that just isn't possible. Here's what I will say, though, as soon as your baby is old enough for it to be possible: please try to prioritize sleep. It's so tempting to finally be able to scroll through the *New York Times* or whatever it might be when you get a moment to yourself, but the lack of sleep will catch up to you. Instead of finding those twenty or thirty minutes at night, see if you can find them during the day somewhere. Keeping yourself on your own priority list also means not pushing yourself to your absolute limit constantly. I'll never do an overnight trip to London again. If you've made your decision to travel, then do it in a somewhat sane way.

When my second child, Ranik, was born, I did things differently. I took a full five months of maternity leave, rarely checked email, and asked people to call me only if something was going terribly wrong. When he was six months old, the COVID pandemic hit, and we no longer had help with child care. Instead of trying to grind through the situation, I pushed back deadlines so that I could take care of the baby—and myself.

But back in 2017, despite not feeling 100 percent like myself, I was giving 100 percent to nVision, and I had results to show for it. We had five different companies investigating us at a rapid clip. Two companies had fallen off because the verbal offers they gave us weren't compelling enough. If I was going to give up running nVision, I had to first believe that the company would do right by the product. But the number also had to be high enough to make my employees (and myself) happy, of course. I kept thinking of Jesus's kids and their college tuition.

Rak asked all the interested companies to place their bids right before Christmas, which is how we ended up getting the offer from Boston Scientific on Shreyas's first birthday. $275 million. $275 million! I had always dreamed of starting my own company, of improving women's health, of doing something big, despite so much doubt around me, but this was more than I ever imagined. This would change my life. Other people's lives. And, I hoped, save lives. Commence sliding to the floor.

But now you know, I stayed on the floor not only because I was shocked and happy, but because I was too tired to take a victory lap.

8

Scale Yourself

The Most Important Product Is You

I might have been too tired for a victory lap when I initially signed the deal to sell the company, but the team deserved one. And finally, when the deal closed four months later, we went for it. We took over the patio at the local Mexican spot around the corner, taking full advantage of the spring sun and cucumber jalapeño margaritas. As the sun set, we decided to return to the office and break into the bottles of tequila we kept stored there.

We were glad we went back, because folks kept showing up as a surprise to celebrate with us. Through the window, I watched Andrew Cleeland as he pulled his car into the parking lot and then ran out to greet him. We gave each other a bear hug. It felt great to celebrate this milestone with him because he had helped me navigate complex negotiations and kept me going when conversations with the larger companies were bumpy. Andrew went to his backseat and pulled out bottles and bottles of Dom Pérignon. Right after him, our attorney, Jake Schwarz, who had helped us form the company and been our lead counsel through the entire deal, showed up with yet another bottle of champagne. Oof, it was going to be that type of night. I don't know how we got there, but there are videos of us dancing to Pharrell Williams's "Happy" barefoot.

Though we signed the term sheet for the sale of nVision in December of 2017, Boston Scientific's acquisition of nVision for $275 million didn't go through until April 15, 2018. When the deal closed, every employee, investor, advisor—anyone who held equity in nVision—had money wired to their bank account. It's a funny thing to stare reality in the face, in black-and-white numbers, and simply not believe what you're seeing. Here I was, the kid who played with bugs, who was always either too brown or not brown enough, a woman, relatively young at thirty-two, and along with an amazing but small team of investors and employees, we pulled it off. Hell yes.

The next evening, two of the Boston Scientific employees who led due diligence on nVision flew from Boston to San Francisco to celebrate in person. Jenny Lee and Scott Sanders were from the marketing and sales groups, respectively. Even before we started working together, I knew they were sharp because of the questions they asked during the diligence phase, which lasted almost a year from the first meeting to the deal closing. At one point, Scott asked to use the device in a model of the fallopian tubes and uterus, and to our surprise, he was able to deploy the balloon correctly the very first time he tried. They were a perfect match for us—thorough, sincere workaholics who also loved to joke around.

On that night, we tucked into Octavia, one of my favorite Michelin-starred restaurants, and devoured all the courses on the prix fixe and what felt like bottomless champagne. We talked about how happy we were that the transaction went through and the impact it could have on patients. We shared photos of our kids. We spent hours and hours together, but we still wanted more time. I was delighted that they would be part of the effort to bring the product to market.

It wasn't all play. Boston Scientific didn't waste any time getting to the serious work of integrating our company into theirs. Two days after the deal closed, the general manager of the entire division, Jeannette Bankes, visited our San Bruno office. The day before, Jeannette had asked me to prepare a presentation that would get her up to speed. In effect, she would be the new CEO of nVision. It wasn't the most comfortable position for me. Someone else would be calling the shots. Who would be good enough? I generally hated the idea of anyone taking over.

But it was hard to dislike Jeannette. She's outgoing, charismatic, and works around the clock. She was genuinely excited about being in our tiny offices, meeting us, and seeing what we were working on. She was delighted when we brought out an nVision hoodie for her as a gift. Though she had worked for a large corporation for a long time and had risen through the ranks of the leadership, she wasn't stuffy. We went to dinner after the meeting, at a Mediterranean place close to the airport. My team saved Jeannette a seat at the center of the table. When she arrived, she insisted that she trade with me, putting herself at the very end. Her goal was never to be the center of attention. Instead, she was focused on being a damn good operator and committed to do the best for any project she was on.

She never thought of me as less capable because of my small company background. In fact, when the commercial lead for nVision was transferred to another position within Boston Scientific, Jeannette asked me to step in to head our effort to launch the product. Jeannette also invited me to come out to Boston and speak at the company's quarterly business review, an important event for them, and I felt honored. I presented the details of what nVision was working on and our most recent clinical data, and my talk received an enthusiastic round of applause and people came up to me after, wanting to meet me or ask me questions. Though Boston Scientific's headquarters had a more corporate atmosphere than our small offices everyone was welcoming and excited about the acquisition.

I was also getting attention outside of Boston Scientific. Rakesh invited me to a dinner with other medical device CEOs, which took place in a private room at Quince in San Francisco. One CEO, Adam Elsesser of Penumbra, couldn't stop talking about a talented female engineer. Feeling drunk on confidence because of the acquisition, and tired of being one of the only women in the room, I said, "I see you feel the need to talk about the one female engineer you hired."

That earned me an invitation to his office, and after a multi-hour conversation, I learned that Adam had started Penumbra in 2004, right after selling a different company to Boston Scientific, and took Penumbra all the way through IPO to a value of $10 billion in 2022. He did this not by hiring one female engineer but many—women comprise 50 percent of his international workforce. We shared our stories, and though we came from vastly different backgrounds, we had much in common. By the end of the meeting, he asked if I would consider joining his board (once interviewed by the rest of the team, of course). I had to pinch myself: in the past few years, I had gone from a million noes while trying to fundraise with a slide deck and a dream to sitting on a public company board led by a CEO whom I admired.

I was equally excited when Mike Mahoney, chairman and CEO of Boston Scientific, asked to meet with me. We had lunch at the company's cafeteria, and though I'm not sure he noticed, every head turned to catch a glimpse of him as he walked by. We chose similar meals, a soup and salad, and settled in to talk about nVision. I was surprised at how much detail he knew—not just about what we did at the company, but also the potential risks as we moved forward. He also listened to what I was most worried about. As with Jeannette, I felt nothing but respect. He even invited me to join the next cocktail reception he was hosting for the board.

Under Mike, Boston Scientific had grown to a company valued at $60 billion and was named one of the best places to work time and time again. He was known to set tough deadlines and expected thought-out answers to pointed questions. But he also aimed to create a nurturing, fun place to work. I remember feeling moved by a LinkedIn post of him raising a LGBT flag over campus. As he talked about his vision for the company, we both got a bit emotional. While many women I worked with already exhibited these qualities, I couldn't help but hope that Andrew, Adam, and Mike were the future of male leadership in this country. Leaders unafraid of their own emotions, unafraid of caring about their employees. Eventually, I met everyone, from the heads of R&D and reimbursement to those on the ground making the gears turn. I felt good about my decision to sell to Boston Scientific.

Though everyone had the best intentions, mergers and acquisitions are never easy for either company, the one acquiring or the one being acquired. At a startup, you're able to get things done more quickly than a corporation with strict processes and layers of management. At large corporations, bureaucracy often exists for a reason. A single mistake could impact millions of customers and cost billions of dollars; a mistake at a startup happens on a much smaller scale. Even though we understood the reason for the red tape, we weren't used to it.

My team still reported to me, and I reported to Jeannette. We all had the same roles as before, but now we had additional responsibilities in the form of training team members from Boston Scientific. No one knew the nVision history like we did, from our clinical trial planning to how to actually build the device. It took more than six months to pass on the institutional knowledge that we had.

At this time, I struggled to understand what we would be responsible for and what Boston Scientific would do, such as who controlled the clinical trial that we were about to launch. After much back-and-forth discussion, we were able to give input, but they were going to take control of the trial. Slowly, they took over every functional area. Wendy, who had been through an acquisition previously, described it like watching the Tour de France: a bicyclist might break out in front of the pack for a while, but eventually, the mob behind them catches up. The original nVision team and I realized that we would have little influence over the destiny of the product. The Boston Scientific team now knew the product well enough, and they knew the Boston Scientific way of doing things better than we did.

No matter what you do, eventually, you have to leave your great passion behind. Maybe life provides you with other priorities, or someday, you retire. And sometimes you're forced to let go before you're ready. However it happens, letting go is especially hard when you've been doubted the whole time you were building your ladder. You have something to prove. As a result, whatever you were striving for becomes so deeply embedded in your identity that it's hard to separate your passion from your person. Somewhat reluctantly, after being at Boston Scientific for two years, I realized that I needed to start thinking about my next chapter. After all, you are your most important product, the one that you need to scale, not whatever you happen to be working on at any given point in time.

For so long—my teenage years and pretty much my entire career—I had remained so focused on my dream of nVision that it was almost impossible to see beyond it. Imagine thinking about a company or product all day every day for years. It takes a lot of time to let go of that. You almost have to reestablish your identity. A big part of what made you is gone.

Then an email hit my inbox I couldn't quite shake. A mutual acquaintance introduced me to a partner at Y Combinator (YC), Jared Friedman. Y Combinator is a storied accelerator, a type of venture investor that also offers mentorship, and had done more for the tech startup ecosystem than any other institution of which I was aware. They were the first investors in and helped launch Airbnb, DoorDash, Instacart, and more than one hundred other companies valued at over a billion dollars. But their reputation and what they've done for Silicon Valley far outstrips any monetary reward. They made startups about entrepreneurs again. While most investors tried to replace the original founders, YC believes that people with technical backgrounds can be great leaders. No MBA required. One of the founders of Y Combinator, Paul Graham, wrote a series of blogs and essays that espouse this ethos and have been read millions of times across the globe.

Jared's email described the company's desire to hire its first health care–focused partner, and he believed my background made me a good fit for the position. Would I consider doing some consulting with them to see if it could work?

Would I? Was I at the point where I could flip the script and use everything I learned in service to others? Had I even "made it" enough to be on the other side of this? A gatekeeper? A wish granter? Was I ready?

Screw it. It was too compelling an opportunity to pass up. Too meaningful an opportunity to let my own doubts, or the doubts of others, get in the way.

In the same room where I fell to the floor in disbelief when I sold the company—in shock at my own worth, in awe of what we had done—I now sat down at my desk, exhaled a deep breath, and replied. I said yes. Because the biggest thing I've learned, without a doubt, is that if you don't try, you can't make anything happen. It was time to bring that message to others.

Conclusion

When I graduated college, I wanted to accomplish three things. First, I wanted to improve women's health. Second, I wanted to elevate the position of women in the corporate world. And third, I wanted to encourage people to think outside the box instead of being tied to whatever society outlines for us. Now I have a job that allows me to do all three.

I am the first group partner at YC with a background in health care. But even getting to YC was a long and winding road. And coinciding with that journey was a parallel path of ups and downs with nVision in its new home. During nVision's clinical trial, it became evident that more patients would need to be enrolled than originally expected, which meant more time and money before the product could be launched. At the same time, the pandemic hit, and enrolling in clinical studies became harder to do. All companies across the board realized they needed to reduce spending on R&D. The nVision device was a casualty of this. Though Boston Scientific could wait for the right time to develop the device further and take it through clinical trials, as of this writing, it is sitting on their shelf.

When I first heard the news, I couldn't breathe. It was like someone had ripped out a piece of my heart. A piece of what made me who I was, what got me out of bed every morning. It was years of work, millions of dollars, dozens of barriers knocked down. And patients really need something like this. But now I have faith that the product will one day be developed, when we're in less uncertain times. And in the meantime, I've found other ways, even bigger ways, to contribute to women's health.

YC knows that the field is important, and I have no limit to how many women's health companies I can invest in, nor is there a limit to the number of women that I can support. In fact, last year, in 2021, I believe I seed funded more women's health–related companies than any other single entity.

One of those companies is Veera Health, started by Shashwata Narain and Shobhita Narain in India. It's a telemedicine platform meant to tackle polycystic ovarian syndrome (PCOS). I also invested in an ovarian cancer diagnostic company, AOA. Oriana Papin-Zoghbi and her cofounding team have already started and sold a company together, so in their second company, they take the problem of early detection seriously; I've rarely met a more thorough team. When they asked me to join their board, I couldn't resist. Our meetings that are scheduled for thirty minutes often end up being hours long, as I impart as much of my knowledge of the problem that I can. I also sit on the board of YourChoice Therapeutics, which will soon have a birth control pill *for men* on the market—something I consider a serious women's health issue. With *Roe v. Wade* dismantled, this product is more important than ever, and the founders have truly found their good indignation.

Outside of YC, founders working on women's health issues

continually reach out to me. Sometimes they want advice, but other times, they just want to say thanks. Every time they go out to fundraise for their companies, they tell me how they use nVision as an example of a successful exit in women's health, making it easier to convince the VC they are talking with to invest. I've also noticed that there are more venture funds dedicated to investing in women's health, like Avestria and Portfolia, which also used my name and nVision when fundraising from their limited partners (people and institutions that put money into venture funds). Investing in women's health is going through a renaissance, and I can only hope that I served as a small part of the movement. Even though the product I worked on for years isn't yet on the market, perhaps I made it easier for others to bring their products forward and help female patients.

I am proud to be part of an endeavor that has been supporting founders who think differently in any field. When I was an entrepreneur, I was totally focused on nVision and the scope of work we were doing. I never had a broad, overarching perspective of entrepreneurship. YC gives me the opportunity to learn about a wide variety of ideas, from spacetech to climatetech to internet startups. It might be an underwater mining company from Europe, or another social app from Palo Alto, or a lending startup out of Nigeria. You never know what you are going to get, but you know it isn't going to be boring.

YC runs two "batches" a year, in summer and in winter. Out of fourteen thousand applications for each batch, YC chooses only two hundred fifty to four hundred companies in which to invest. Before the batch starts, we interview thousands of companies for ten minutes each. I was skeptical of the process at first.

How much can you really learn about a company in ten minutes? It turns out, a whole lot: How eloquent is the founder? How do they react to pressure? Do they know their numbers like the backs of their hands? YC expects many of the same things I expected from myself when I was running nVision—thoroughness, thinking quickly on your feet, and above all, building something people want—and in the case of health care companies, often something people need.

When the batch starts, I get to work with amazing entrepreneurs. No politics; they just want to build their companies. Because of the pandemic, our meetings happen on Zoom, but that doesn't stop me from really connecting with the founders. And the more time I spent with founders, the more I fell in love with the job. I work with seasoned entrepreneurs like Jessica Jackley, the founder of Kiva.org, who then started another company, Alltruists, a subscription for at-home, kid-friendly volunteer projects for families, which appeals to the mom in me. Jessica often has one of her three kids in the background or even on her lap when we meet, and that doesn't stop us from getting shit done. I worked with first-time founders like Aadit Palicha and Kaivalya Vohra, who are building Zepto, which provides fifteen-minute grocery delivery in India. I remember when they first launched out of Mumbai, I told them to go celebrate, and they had to remind me that they were too young to drink at eighteen and nineteen years old!

On the health care side of things, we invested in Biodock, a software that uses artificial intelligence to interpret scientific images of cells, which later went on to raise significant money from powerhouse venture capital firm Andreessen Horowitz. And

Nuntius Therapeutics, a female-run company working on gene therapy for currently incurable muscle-related diseases.

But my favorite time isn't when we see what ends up being successful—although that is rewarding—it's when we first get started. To kick off the batch, I always share my own entrepreneurial story the most honest way I know how. I make sure not to skip any of the hard parts, because I want to share with them everything I went through and did wrong, in the hopes that other people with a big dream, and surely a big cast of doubters, take away something from it. They hear me and reciprocate by coming to me with their highs and lows.

So, in addition to all of the operational problems I help founders tackle, I spend a good deal of time talking to founders about the various emotions that they're going through. As they are turned down by both potential investors and employees, I tell them to screw the doubters.

But I also tell them about the doubter that is hardest to jettison. Reflecting on my experience, I've learned that the most important doubt to overcome is self-doubt. You'll never be able to please everyone or make them see your worth. If you sell a company for $275 million, someone will call you a one-hit wonder. If you sell the next one for a billion, someone will say you got lucky. You will always have doubters and even haters. Haters are gonna hate. Let that doubt fuel you. But be kind to yourself. The trick to success is not to doubt yourself too much. To know your own worth. Taking care of yourself is a demonstration that you do know your worth. All that being said, not even the most successful entrepreneurs I know, the ones who have built billion-dollar companies, are without any doubts.

I'm in no way advising that you get rid of all of your self-doubt. I don't know how one goes about doing that, and I don't know if I would get rid of all of mine even if I could. After all, those who are without a doubt must not be very self-aware. It's our self-doubt that keeps us honest, humble. It helps us to know where we have room for improvement and when to be alert to risks around the corner that we need to pay attention to.

Though we may never be, nor should we be, free of all doubt, we shouldn't ever be defeated by it. It's an art to keep doubt in its place, and wield it—both others' and our own—as necessary. The most damaging thing doubt can do is prevent you from trying, from building your own ladder. Go ahead and take that step. Maybe you'll fall on the floor. I like your chances.

Acknowledgments

I hope that it's clear from reading this book that it takes more than the founder to bring a company to life. Both professionally and personally.

I would like to start by thanking my nVision Familia. We wouldn't have had the exit we did, but even more important, we wouldn't have had the experience, the fun, the everyday reward that we did without this dynamic, fierce group of people.

Katherine Macway, thank you for your warmth and consistent good work. I still can't believe you came to us straight out of school; you outperformed your years of experience. Alan Bradley, thanks for always keeping a fire in your belly and for your thoroughness, cleverness, and organization. Mika Nishimura, thank you for never thinking any task was too small to take on, for being so hardworking and willing to take any flight at any time, and for thinking through some of our greatest challenges. Christina Skieller, thank you for your brilliant engineering work, your healthy skepticism, and your love of doing everything in a greener way. Wendy Heigel, thank you for your tireless work, dedication to our cause, willingness to try anything for the first time, and confidence in the face of adversity, and for your friendship. Dave Snow, thank you for jump-starting my career, for the multitude of lessons and stories we've collected over the years, for the indescribably important work you did on the nVision device, and for your friendship. Jesus Magana, thank you for your warmth and hard work, for taking the work so seriously but never taking yourself too seriously. Dr. Albert Chin and Serge Bierhuizen, thank you for your engineering prowess and constantly innovating in the face of setbacks. Kevin O'Conner, thank you for all of your keen insights into the women's health market and the instrumental introductions you made to physicians. Cindy Domecus, you are a regulatory ninja and I learned so much from you; thank you.

The Bhandarkars, thank you for believing in me, showing me love and support, always welcoming me into your beautiful home, and making the first, most important connections for the company. Mallika, even at twelve, you were wise beyond your years and sheltered me from preteen hormone-induced storms. Poornima Kumar, thank you for meeting with me, brainstorming the name of the company, and throwing in your keen insights and valuable connections.

Jake Schwarz, when we first met at that café in Redwood City, I had absolutely no idea what I was doing. You took a risk on me and incorporated the company anyway. I'll never forget your explanation of how fundraising works and the type of characters to watch out for. Even today, I am comforted by the fact that you are in my corner.

Anula Jayasuriya, thank you for not only believing in me from the start but also pushing me to my limits. It allowed me to see my own potential. I became tougher under your mentorship and loved trying to exceed your already very high expectations.

When things got hard, professionally and personally, I always knew I could turn to you. I know that's something that holds true today. Karen Drexler, you were always the balanced voice of reason, plainly stating your opinion on any subject that came up. Because of that, I always felt like I could rely on you. Thank you.

Corinne Nevinny, thanks for taking the risk on me and on women's health. Instead of letting the lack of great comps in women's health deter you, it drew you in. You felt like you had a responsibility toward women's health before "femtech" was the hot topic of the day, and I am so glad for our first two rainy encounters. Thank you, Linda Greub and Margot Shapiro, for making the LMN VC investment in nVision.

Darshana Zaveri, it's been quite the journey together. The book said it all: thank you for trusting my instincts, believing that I had operational ability, not passion alone. Tasneem Dohadwala and the Excelestar family, thank you for the meaningful conversations we had in the early days, and your investment and support until the end.

Tuff Yen, Peter Truwit, and the Seraph Group, you are my favorite type of investors—trusting and endlessly supportive. Gwen Edwards and Golden Seeds, raising money from you is a right of passage for a female entrepreneur, and thank you for everything you do for the ecosystem. Faz Bashi and the Life Science Angels, thank you for your commitment to our field and for investing before we had any real proof of concept. You connected me to everyone you knew to get our Series A done, and I'm so grateful for it. Ted Kuh and the Berkeley Angel Network—go Bears! Thank you for your support and your thoughtful feedback on this book.

Fred St. Goar, I know how hard you worked and how much you put on the line to get me into the Fogarty Innovation. You've been one of my biggest supporters, and thank you especially for being a champion of the nVision pivot into detecting cancer.

John Mittelstet and Donna Butcher, though we became close during the worst of times, and we miss Sharron every day, I am thankful for our friendship and for your belief in me.

Ms. Anita Chetty and Ms. Joanne Mason, thank you for your steadfast belief in me and all of your support during my most trying high school years.

Tom Shehab and Jan Garfinkle, what you've built at Arboretum is simply incredible, and I am glad that you were part of the nVision journey. I'm lucky that you think for yourselves and didn't wait for Silicon Valley investors to show their enthusiasm.

Sharon Vosmek, thank you for being a most excellent confidant and cheerleader and investor, and for everything you do for women entrepreneurs. Roger Bamford and Joyo Wijaya, you were a major part of our Series A, though nVision was outside of your comfort zone. Thank you for your belief and support.

Tim Draper, thank you for seeing me and my potential and what the company could be, and being the first man to do so. I continue to watch you and learn from you, and I admire the way you stand up for what you believe in and aren't afraid of big ideas, no matter what less-creative people have to say about it.

Thank you to Deborah Kilpatrick and Amy Belt Raimundo for not only offering invaluable advice through the years but for starting MedtechWomen. It filled this once-young female engineer's heart full of hope to see all of the women leaders in our industry when I attended one of your conferences years ago. Thank you to Josh Makower and Paul Yock for taking my calls over the years, but also for writing the *Biodesign* textbook, which became my bible in the early days of the company. Adeyemi Ajao, the greatest teacher of how to fundraise of all time. You unleashed a power I didn't know I had, and today I try to pass that gift on to others.

Cami Samuels and Vineeta Agarwal, the advice that you gave me during your diligence process informed many decisions I made regarding nVision and what I did afterward. Thank you.

To all of the physicians who supported nVision, who believed that their patients deserved something more, thank you: Bethan Powell, Vivian Connor, Ted Anderson, Andrew Brill, Amy Garcia, Jose Garza, Ronny Drapkin, Sarah Kim, Charles Landen, Carol Cooke, Lynn Westphal, Sharmila Pramanik, and countless others.

To all of the ovarian cancer patients and women who are at high risk for developing ovarian cancer who reached out to me: it pained me to hear what you were going through, your lack of options, but it fueled me to push on the many times I thought I was out of gas. Thank you for sharing your stories.

Andrew Cleeland, spending time with you had a remarkable impact on both the nVision outcome and the type of leader I am today. As I now advise other entrepreneurs, all of the conversations we had are top of mind. Rakesh Mehta, you once stood outside of Whole Foods for an hour trying to calm me down after an especially bad meeting with a potential acquirer. Thank you for being my right hand during the most exciting, stress-inducing experience of my life—the nVision acquisition.

Jared Friedman, thank you for introducing me to YC. You

ACKNOWLEDGMENTS

are one of the most intelligent, hardworking people I've had the pleasure to work with, and that's saying something. Thank you to the group partners at YC for the lessons and laughs over the years, for believing I had what it takes to join your ranks, and for demonstrating that it is truly possible to stay grounded and humble even after great success: Michael Seibel, Dalton Caldwell, Brad Flora, Nicolas Dessaigne, Gustaf Alströmer, Aaron Epstein, Diana Hu, and Harj Taggar. Let's keep putting founders first. Paul Graham and Jessica Livingston and the other founders of YC, it's an honor to carry forward what you've created. Geoff Ralston and Garry Tan, thank you for your leadership. To every founder I've worked with, you've chosen one of the hardest, if not the hardest, path—and it's an honor to try to help you where I can. Kat Mañalac, thank you for all of the help with this book; it's been such a pleasure to work with you, and I know it will continue to be.

Oh, to put the whole nVision journey in a book! Another startup in itself, with so many people throwing their weight behind it. Carol Mann, not only did you believe my story would make a good book, but in almost every conversation we have, I can sense that you want to improve the state of women's health and women in business. Stephanie Frerich, every time we spoke it would inspire my writing. I'm so lucky to have found an editor who shares some of my good indignations. Thank you for picking up this book and investing your precious time in it. Dawn Davis, Emily Simonson, Brittany Adames, and everyone at Simon & Schuster who worked on this book: I didn't know what a process this was going to be, but I am so happy to have had such a wonderful team to work with. Karen Kelly, thank you for your humor. Sara Corbett, thank you for thinking about the best way to frame the advice and story in this book, while trying to teach me some Writing 101. I think of our few months together often and fondly.

Carlye Adler, it's clear that you see the best in the authors whom you work with, as it is reflected on the page. It was so special, and such an honor, to work so closely with you on this book after devouring so much of your other work. I'm not sure I've ever worked with someone less judgmental or more kind than you are. Thank you for your creative, thorough work, your patience, and somehow always making the time.

Oh, my girlfriends. Where would I be without all of you? From preteen angst and family drama to raising families of our own, I'm so lucky to have you with me. Doors always open, arms always open wide, you are the best of the best.

Julia Gitis, you loved me enough to tell me you didn't think signing a book deal was a good idea while I was pregnant and recovering from selling the company, but read drafts of it anyway. And that's after reading my college applications in high school and nVision's very first business plan. When I was in the hospital after my water broke, you showed up almost every day for weeks, despite the thirty-minute drive each way. You are intelligent and hilarious and a good person through and through. My life is made better—more stable, more full, more fun, more comfortable—with you in it. Thank you, and I love you.

Deborah Tu, it's been a while since we ran through the hallways of my parents' house with all of the lights off, leaping down stairs without knowing where our feet would fall. Now here we are, in San Francisco with our budding families. Thanks for always encouraging me to prioritize my health, even when I didn't listen, for your hilarious sarcasm, and for celebrating our birthdays together every year, no matter what.

Opal Kamdar, they say it's important to have a doctor in the family, so thank goodness my sister is one (that's you). I still can't believe that when I was in the hospital with Shreyas, and I felt scared and unsure, you packed your bags and flew across the country without much discussion. Life is in a good spot, both of ours, but I know that tough times are inevitably ahead, and when they come, I know it's just as inevitable that we'll be there for each other. Thank you.

Kim Shottan, thank you for assembling our stroller and creating the list of everything we needed for the baby while I was in the hospital. Also, your dedication to your own family is an example to us all, and I'm so lucky to be on this motherhood journey with you. And thank you for making your friends my friends, and the life-changing trip to Oregon we took with them.

Prerna Sethi, my friend with impeccable style and such a unique sense of aesthetics. Thank you for accepting the fact that I get dressed in the dark but also offering to go shopping for me. You made me feel more confident as I was transitioning into corporate American life. When I'm with you, it's clear that you adore my quirkiness, which encourages me to be me. Now, seeing you with your baby girl fills my heart with love and joy.

Chrissy Bertolli, they say it's tough to find close friends after graduating college. Clearly, there are exceptions. We met as my parents were starting their divorce, and I don't know what I would have done without your guidance, love, and support through it. When my water broke early, and I was in the hospital, you not only designed our nursery but waited for packages to arrive. How can I say thank you for something like that? Also, it's so fun to be in your company. I miss our random daytime beers, and maybe they'll return when our kiddos are a bit older.

Vaishali Bhardwaj, our moms were pregnant together, then pushed us in strollers side by side, and now my kiddo has blown out poop diapers while you held him, and I can't wait to spoil your daughter. If you and I didn't take good enough care of our friendship when we were younger, we're making up for it in spades now. Thank you for your pragmatism and optimism, willingness to try new things, and sense of adventure and humor, and for being there to celebrate.

Aruna Bharati, thank you for your intelligence and humor and for creating nVision's first logo, and for being a bigger person than I am sometimes able to be. Thank you, Sophia Wang, for showing me, at such an early age, that great accomplishment and intelligence don't need to come with bragging or ego. Sheena Vaswani, you've had to show unmatched strength in this life and I both admire and adore you for it. Erika Stanzl and Kate Garret, I'm so glad that we could be the only women in the room some-times, much better than being the only woman.

Andrew Schwartz and Shabnam Aggarwal, I knew nothing about how to go about writing and publishing a book when I reached out to you, and you were generous and patient with your time. Thank you. I hope the two of you keep writing and writing.

To the entire Behera clan, especially Mamata and Kirtan, how lucky I am that Raj made me part of your family. Thank you for always supporting the career of your daughter-in-law.

Swasti, my beautiful little sister, you were my very first baby.

I would nurture you and love on you starting from a young age, but how quickly the tables turned. When we were little girls, every weekend we would go to a different Indian friend's house, and the moms would set up art competitions. They would pick a different art project for us to do, and when we were done, they would make all the little girls vote on who had done the best job. One day, the assigned art project was decorating your own plastic visor with paint. I really messed mine up. I tried to paint an *S* and it somehow looked like an *M*. When it was time to vote, the girls started snickering and no one voted for me. I couldn't even vote for myself. But then I turned around, and there you were, holding your hand high above your head. Swasti, you believed in me and saw my potential before anyone else did. Thank you.

Mom, Anupama Sarna, I've tried so many different ways of showing my gratitude. And each time I do, I fall short. Because there is no way for me to express the limitless amount of thanks I have in my heart for you. If I could somehow become half the mom you are, it would be an achievement that outshines any found in this book.

Rajeev, I couldn't have pulled through the toughest years of nVision without you. You were my de facto cofounder, talking me through every difficult decision, keeping me in the saddle when things got hard. I loved the years we spent, side by side on our laptops, furiously working away into the wee hours. Now, it's our kiddos keeping us up, and I wouldn't have it any other way. I love you. To my kiddos, my little boys Ranik and Shreyas, I love you three and six infinities. Thank you for making me a mamma, for expanding the spectrum of emotions that I feel. For making me a happier, more balanced person. You are the greatest joy I've ever known.

Notes

1. A GOOD INDIGNATION
Finding a Problem You Want to Work On

24 *When it came to ovarian cancer*: William H. Parker, Vanessa Jacoby, Donna Shoupe, and Walter Rocca, "Effect of Bilateral Oophorectomy on Women's Long-Term Health," *Women's Health* 5, no. 5 (2009): 565–76, https://doi .org/10.2217/whe.09.42.

24 *When it came to ovarian cancer, I learned that each year*: U.S. Cancer Statistics Working Group, "United States Cancer Statistics: Data Visualizations," Centers for Disease Control and Prevention, accessed September 21, 2022, https://gis.cdc.gov/Cancer/USCS/#!Trends/.

24 *Even so, only 20 percent of ovarian cancer cases*: Joan Hartnett, Bridgette Thom, and Nancy Kline, "Caregiver Burden in End-Stage Ovarian Cancer," *Clinical Journal of Oncology Nursing* 20, no. 2 (April 2016): 169–73, https: doi:10.1188/16.CJON.169-173.

24 *Other serious conditions that impact women*: Sanjay K. Agarwal et al., "Clinical Diagnosis of Endometriosis: A Call to Action," *American Journal of Obstetrics &*

Gynecology 220, no. 4 (April 1, 2019): 354.e1–54.e12, https://doi.org/10.1016/j.ajog.2018.12.039.

24 *More than one uterus a minute*: "Hysterectomy Options," Brigham and Women's Hospital, accessed August 5, 2022, https://www.brighamandwomens.org/obgyn/minimally -invasive-gynecologic-surgery/hysterectomy-options.

24 *And one of the leading causes of infertility*: Olubukola AT Omidiji et al. "Hysterosalpingographic Findings in Infertility—What Has Changed over the Years?" *African Health Sciences* 19, no. 2 (June 2019): 1866–74, https://doi .org/10.4314/ahs.v19i2.9.

2. BUILDING YOUR OWN LADDER
Gaining the Right Experience

29 *He also started to learn coding when*: Cory Althoff, "The Coding Education of Kevin Systrom: Creator of Insta- gram," *Self-Taught*, February 8, 2018, accessed July 15, 2022, https://selftaught.blog/coding-education-of-kevin-systrom -instagram/.

34 *Almost 50 percent of the US population*: American Heart Association News, "Cardiovascular Diseases Affect Nearly Half of American Adults, Statistics Show," American Heart Association, January 31, 2019, accessed July 15, 2022, https://www.heart.org/en/news/2019/01/31/cardiovas cular-diseases-affect-nearly-half-of-american-adults-statis tics-show. See also: Centers for Disease Control and Preven- tion, National Center for Health Statistics, "Multiple Cause of Death, 1999–2020," CDC WONDER Online Database,

accessed February 21, 2022, https://wonder.cdc.gov/wonder
/help/mcd.html/; C. W. Tsao et al. "Heart Disease and Stroke
Statistics—2022 Update: A Report from the American
Heart Association," *Circulation* 145, vol. 8 (February 22,
2022): e153–e639; National Center for Chronic Disease Prevention and Health Promotion, Division for Heart Disease
and Stroke Prevention, "Heart Disease Facts," Centers for
Disease Control and Prevention, accessed July 15, 2022,
https://www.cdc.gov/heartdisease/facts.htm.

3. WHILE YOU'RE DOWN THERE
Networking Without a Network

48 *That's a legit theory that Microsoft researchers*: David Smith,
"Proof! Just Six Degrees of Separation Between Us," *Guard-
ian*, August 2, 2008, accessed July 15, 2022, https://www
.theguardian.com/technology/2008/aug/03/internet.email.

50 *That's why, as soon as we sat down at the café*: "Video: HSG
Test for Female Infertility," Mayo Clinic, accessed October 31,
2022, https://www.mayoclinic.org/hsg-test/vid-20084751.

58 *This question compelled me to dig deeper*: Reuters,
"Merck to Spin Off Women's Health and Biosimilar
Drugs, Focus on Keytruda," CNBC, February 5, 2020, accessed August 5, 2022, https://www.cnbc.com/2020/02/05
/merck-says-it-plans-to-spin-off-its-slow-growth-pro
ducts-into-a-new-company.html?&qsearchterm=merck
%20to%20spin%20off%20woman.

59 *Gynecologists often get sued*: Jennifer Sangalang, Holly
Baltz, and John Pacenti, "Average OB-GYN Faces 2 or 3

Lawsuits During a Career. This Palm Beach County Doctor Had 9," *Palm Beach Post*, September 23, 2021, accessed August 5, 2022, https://www.palmbeachpost.com/story/news/2021/09/23/florida-doctor-medical-malpractice-lawsuits-women-babies-died/8336090002.

6. SHIT HAPPENS

Keep Going Through Life's Ups and Downs

147 *Today, only about 13 percent of venture capitalists*: Neal Dempsey, "Venture Capital Is Still a 'Boys' Club.' Let's Start to Change That," *Crunchbase News*, August 17, 2021, accessed August 5, 2022, https://news.crunchbase.com/venture/venture-capital-female-gender-diversity/.

7. LETTING GO

Knowing When to Make a Change

175 *American workers across the board saw heightened rates of burnout in 2021*: "The American Workforce Faces Compounding Pressure: APA's 2021 Work and Well-Being Survey Results," American Psychological Association, accessed October 28, 2022, https://www.apa.org/pubs/reports/work-well-being/compounding-pressure-2021.

176 *Meanwhile, 36 percent reported cognitive weariness*: Ashley Abramson, "Burnout and Stress Are Everywhere," American Psychological Association, *Monitor on Psychology* 53, no. 1, January 1, 2022, accessed August 5, 2022, https://www.apa.org/monitor/2022/01/special-burnout-stress.

About the Author

Surbhi Sarna is an entrepreneur, partner at Y Combinator, advocate for innovation in health care, and investor. She worked as an engineer before becoming CEO and founder of nVision Medical. nVision developed a catheter-based device for early detection of ovarian cancer and, after obtaining FDA clearance, was purchased by Boston Scientific. Sarna also sits on both nonprofit and for-profit company boards, has been featured in *Bloomberg/Businessweek*, *Forbes*, *Entrepreneur*, and *Inc.*, and has received numerous awards, including being named on the *Forbes* 30 Under 30 list and the *Inc.* Female Founders 100 list. She lives in San Francisco with her husband and two children.